Central and Eastern European Economies

Perspectives and Challenges

Marcus Goncalves and Erika Cornelius Smith

BUSINESS EXPERT PRESS

Central and Eastern European Economies: Perspectives and Challenges

First published in 2016 by
Business Expert Press, LLC
222 East 46th Street, New York, NY 10017
www.businessexpertpress.com

ISBN-13: 978-1-63157-552-5 (paperback)
ISBN-13: 978-1-63157-553-2 (e-book)

Business Expert Press Economics Collection

Collection ISSN: 2163-761X (print)
Collection ISSN: 2163-7628 (electronic)

Cover and interior design by Exeter Premedia Services Private Ltd., Chennai, India

First edition: 2016

10 9 8 7 6 5 4 3 2 1

Printed in the United States of America.

For my International Business students at Nichols College, for the great discussions about regional markets and the global markets as a whole, and for keeping me on my toes; for my beloved wife Carla, always patient and caring with me during these intense projects; for my son Samir, who brings me so much pride; and for my other two children, Andrea and Joshua (in memory), also treasures in my life, for which I count the days to be reunited with. To God be the glory!

Marcus Goncalves

Spring 2016

For my students at Nichols College, who inspire me with their humor and tenacity; for my muses, Sophie and Phoebe, who inspire me with their curiosity and moments of pure joy; and for my spouse, Andrew, who inspires me with his generosity and an abundant supply of strawberry licorice. For all of this and more, I am truly blessed.

Erika Cornelius Smith

Spring 2016

Abstract

This book provides relevant and timing information addressing a significant aspect of the economic, political, and social transition in Central and Eastern Europe (CEE) over the last several decades, integrating historical data with the most recent political and economic reporting based on the author's analysis. Analysis include assessments, opinions, and experience (where appropriate) as scholars, researchers, consultants, and global citizens, from an introduction to the historical context for European integration, including the political structures and economic relationships forged in the post-World War II period, to the relationship between the European Union and the economies of states in CEE, examining the political, economic, and security considerations that complicated the federalist relationship in each state, and end with a brief discussion of the adoption of the euro. This book also discusses the economic impact of integration of CEE countries as they attempt to make their economic transition and to integrate with the European Union and other free-market economies. The authors look at the economic growth and challenges these countries face, as well as how the indebtedness of the advanced economies are impacting these economies and prompting them to launch economic countermeasure to protect their own economies.

Keywords

Central European Economies, CEE, Eastern European Economies, EEE, Eastern Europe, European Union

Contents

Preface

This book is divided into six chapters, each addressing a significant aspect of the economic, political, and social transition in Central and Eastern Europe over the last several decades. We integrate historical data with the most recent political and economic reporting in our analysis, including our assessments, opinions, and experience (where appropriate) as scholars, researchers, consultants, and global citizens.

Chapter 1 provides the reader with an introduction to the historical context for European integration, including the political structures and economic relationships forged in the post-World War II period. We pay close attention to the impact of nationalist histories and geography on the politics of integration, and include brief introductions to each country included in later chapters of this publication.

Chapter 2 focuses more specifically on the relationship between the European Union and the economies of states in Central and Eastern Europe. We examine the political, economic, and security considerations that complicated the federalist relationship in each state, and end with a brief discussion of the adoption of the euro.

Chapter 3 provides an overview of these Eastern European countries in transition from a state-centered economy to a free-market, decentralized one. We provide an overview of the geopolitical and economic challenges of both, the Central and Eastern European bloc and the Commonwealth of Independent States blocs. We also discuss the economic challenges faced by these economies regionally, as well as in consequence of external forces brought by advanced economies, such as the global financial contagion resulted of the economic crisis that started in 2007, as well as currency wars and its consequences to local and global economies.

Chapter 4 discusses the economic impact of integration of CEE countries as they attempt to make their economic transition and to integrate with the European Union and other free-market economies. We look at the economic growth and challenges these countries face, as well as how the indebtedness of the advanced economies are impacting these economies and prompting them to launch economic countermeasure to protect their own economies.

Chapter 5 discusses the many challenges for foreign investors and multinational corporations (MNCs) in entering Eastern European markets, from skill mismatches and educational systems, to the impact of economic restructuring, legal framework, and trading policies. This chapter also provides an overview as to the main reasons why MNCs fail in Eastern Europe markets.

Chapter 6 introduces multiple frameworks for the study of political risk, and provides an overview of this important field for the reader. The chapter proceeds with country-based case studies that include *Freedom House* scores, electoral results, and in-depth political analysis to assess the potential risk created by stable or reforming political institutions in each CEE state.

Extensive, user-friendly appendixes that provide additional country-specific case studies and analysis for the reader follow these chapters. Our hope is that this work will provide an introduction to the historical and political context of the culturally rich, vibrant, and rapidly changing region of Central and Eastern Europe. We have balanced this introduction with breadth and depth for the international business professional who desires to engage in the significant opportunities available to those willing to explore this very important region in transition.

Acknowledgments

There were many people who helped us during the process of writing this book. It would be impossible to keep track of them all. Therefore, to all that we have forgotten to list, please don't hold it against us!

We would like to thank Mr. Bo-Young Lin, from the Graduate Institute of International and Development Studies and United Nations Conference on Trade and Development (UNCTAD) for his support and insights. We would also like to express our appreciation to many corporate leaders who shared their views and experiences with us in the Eastern European region. Our special thanks go to the following leaders and great friends: Jörgen Eriksson, Founding Partner at Bearing Group Ltd, in London, United Kingdom; Ewelina Kroll, Public Relations Manager at East Europe Consulting, in Gdynia, Poland; Piotr Kozicki, Business Information Security Officer at Citigroup Global Fund Services, in Warsaw, Poland; Julius Niedvaras, Director of International Business School at Vilnius University, in Vilnius, Lithuania; Luc Jalllois Sr. VP at LJL Consulting, in Kiev, Ukraine; Galyna Konto, Investment Manager, in Kiev, Ukraine; Markéta Remišovská, Principal at Rizzo Associates, in Praga, Czech Republic; and Dmitriy Lisenkov, Hedge Fund Manager at The Russian Technology Fund, in St. Petersburg, Russia.

CHAPTER 1

The European Context for Integration and Accession

Overview

Nearly seven decades ago, six countries in Western Europe (Belgium, France, West Germany, Italy, Luxembourg, and the Netherlands) decided to take economic cooperation to the next level. The vision of the European Union (EU) founding states, epitomized by the Schuman Declaration in 1950, was to tie their economies—including the re-emerging West German economy—so closely together that war would become impossible.

In 1973, Denmark, Ireland, and the United Kingdom joined what was then referred to as the "European Community." The 1970s were also a decade of deep social and political transformations in Greece, Portugal, and Spain, where military regimes and dictatorships were overthrown. Inspired by the prosperity and stability of the European Community, these countries joined the European project within 10 years, strengthening their emerging democracies. The countries benefited enormously from free trade and common economic policies, in particular structural funds designed to foster convergence by funding infrastructure and investments in poorer regions.

Despite these significant cooperative achievements, the most significant episode in Europe's postwar political and economic integration was symbolized by the fall of the Berlin Wall. A defining moment in the collapse of the centrally planned economic systems of the 1980s, the collapse of the Wall and the Soviet Union ushered in a multifaceted process of liberalization.

On the one hand, the fall of communism broke countries apart, with the dissolution of the Soviet Union and Yugoslavia followed in 1993 by the "Velvet Divorce" of the Czech and Slovak republics. On the other hand, less than a year after the Berlin Wall came down, East and West Germany reunified. More than 20 countries emerged from communism in a new, more democratic Europe. The integration of these states presented both the greatest opportunities and the greatest challenges of the post-World War II era. In this context, this chapter provides the reader with an introduction to the broader context of European integration and accession, with special attentions to economic, political, and social challenges across the region. It concludes with a series of short case studies that introduce the reader to the process of transition in the individual Central and Eastern European (CEE) states.

The Effects of History and Geography on Regional Identity

As depicted in Figure 1.1, several scholars writing about the regions of CEE are faced with the unique challenge of identifying and "naming" a series of states in the process of "a return to Europe." Some who study the region suggest that the "English language lacks an appropriate and widely acceptable collective name" for the regions that form the Balkans and East Central Europe.[1] In German, for example, they are referred to as *Zwischeneuropa* (in between Europe). Global political and economic integration, as well as redefined political communities within each state, present new opportunities to construct communities of belonging. Katalin Fábián[2] writes,

> The Baltic states of Estonia, Latvia, and Lithuania, as well as several stateless people, divided sub-regions, and ethnic, linguistic, and religious minorities (the Russian territory between Ukraine, Poland, Slovakia, Hungary, or Muslims in Bulgaria, for example) keenly illustrate how previously submerged political and cultural identities can re-emerge and create themselves.

---

[1] Bideleux and Jeffries (2007, xiii).
[2] Fábián (2007, 6).

Figure 1.1 CEE political bloc

Source: Kubilius (2016).

As a consequence of these shifting identities and politics, scholars who focus on the study of CEE states struggle with how or what to call this region given the historical context and changing political affiliations.[3] Use of the term "Central Europe" typically refers to Germany and Austria (formally the Central Powers) and excludes the Baltic States and the South Eastern European countries that can be included in an analysis of transition and accession. Use of the term "East Europe" delineates the states from the "West" of Europe in the post-World War II Cold War context and aligns them more closely with the Soviet sphere of influence. Historians, political scientists, economists and other researchers writing about the region emphasize one or the other signifier as a matter of political choice. Geography has very little to do with the choice to

---

[3] Kubilius (2016).

employ Central or Eastern Europe. It is a matter of selective inclusion and exclusion.

With these considerations in mind, our study will cast a broader net by referring to the collective region as CEE, unless referencing a specific organization or regional alliance. This includes the Baltic States (Estonia, Latvia, and Lithuania), Poland, the Czech Republic, Slovakia, Hungary, Romania, Slovenia, Croatia, Bosnia and Herzegovina, Serbia and Montenegro, Bulgaria, Macedonia, and Albania. Other studies of the region integrated the Baltic countries alongside Poland, Hungary, and former Czechoslovakia as part of their analysis of CEE economics and politics because the two areas achieved independent statehood within the eastern zone of Europe between 1918 and 1940.[4]

Global Influences on the Transition

The distinctions in the history and geography that impact "naming" also signal that these states each had very different relationships to communism. Slovenian scholars, for example, protest the use of "post-communism" to describe their state, arguing that the ruling regime was clearly not a true communist system. Rather, "it relied on oppression and never reached the level of material abundance required for this stage of development according to Marxist theory."[5] For this reason, it is important to discuss the broad economic and political trends that influenced the transition of CEE states beyond the fall of the Berlin Wall.

The End of National Planning

Many of the "national economic" models employed after World War II began to pull apart by the 1970s. This included Soviet-style state capitalism, national planning in the West, and import-substitution industrialization in the South. The decade witnessed a "loosening" of capital controls in the United States and Britain, and a deregulation of stock exchanges. These changes "facilitated a spectacular growth and centralization of

---

[4] For examples of these inclusive studies see Crampton (1974).

[5] Humer (2007).

international banking, insurance, and securities markets."[6] The restructuring of finance capital and the deregulation of national capital markets created the first "wave" of the demise of the national planning systems.

It should be noted that from 1973 to 1978, while the Western world experienced economic recession in response to the staggering increases in oil prices of Organization of the Petroleum Exporting Countries (OPEC), the CEE and Eastern Balkan states continued to grow. In some cases, this growth was even faster than the previous decade.[7] Increasing dependency on the Soviet market and imports of underpriced Soviet oil, gas, and power-generating equipment and technology were accompanied by exports of agricultural and manufactured goods back to the Soviet Union. This type of Soviet "assistance" insulated these economies against adverse trading trends and the potentially damaging effects of recession and higher oil prices, but impaired their future capacity to export successfully to the West.

Despite continuing reliance on the Soviet Union, the 1970s East-West détente did facilitate an increase in the flow of Western capital and technology into the CEE economies. Many of the states "eagerly accepted" Western investments, joint ventures, loans, industrial installations, and "technology transfers" as substitutes for fundamentally altering their economic systems.[8] Economic historians note that excessive reliance on increased Western capital technology and firms had two significant consequences for the CEE states: (1) increased contact with Western visitors and products helped to diffuse Western values, consumerism, and pop culture, particularly among younger generations; and (2) reliance on these transfers created equally serious economic hazards.[9] The Westernization of CEE values, dress, leisure activities, and worldviews among young

---

[6] Dale (2011, 11).

[7] Bideleux and Jeffries (2007, 511–12). Two notable exceptions existed at this time: the increasingly nationalist Albanian and Romania communist regimes were denied Soviet "assistance," despite their rapidly diminishing domestic mineral resources. Albania began receiving significant support from China in return for its support of that state during the Sino-Soviet disputes of the 1960s and early 1970s, and at that point no longer participated as an active member in Comecon.

[8] Bideleux and Jeffries (2007, 513).

[9] Stokes (1991).

people living in the region contributed as much to the demise of the communist system as systemic reforms. Through their clumsy attempts to curb the grown influence of rock concerts, Western pop music, blue jeans, and consumerism, the ageing dictators made them seem increasingly old fashioned, puritanical, out of touch and ridiculous, especially in the eyes of the young.[10]

Further, capital and technology transfers created serious economic problems. Debt-service payments were burdensome and drained the much-needed resources for infrastructure. As CEE credit ratings fell in the 1970s, the states had difficulty continuing to import goods, including materials needed for existing Western projects within their states. Jeff Sommers, Jānis Bērziņš, and Adam Fabry[11] argue that financialization and economic globalization were linked as a response to the crises of the mid-1970s.

These factors were further complicated by another slowdown of global economic growth and return of crises in the 1980s. From 1979 to 1983, the economies of the CEE states suffered acute economic recessions. Whereas economists noted per capita annual global growth in the 1960s and 1970s at a rate of roughly 3 percent, the 1980s and beyond have seen a rate of nearly half that amount. In the more extreme cases of Romania and Poland, the economies experienced severe economic contractions and significant reductions in living standards.

The Rise of Neoliberalism

Daniel Gros and Alfred Steinherr[12] championed the progress of CEE states in the mid-1990s, writing, "Like Western Europe after World War II, Eastern European countries now have the historic opportunity to create ex nova optimal economic and social institutions and thereby free their latent energies."[13] Persuaded by the merits of neoliberal ideology, the scholars championed CEE countries potential to "leapfrog those

---

[10] Bideleux and Jeffries (2007, 513).
[11] Sommers and Bērziņš (2011).
[12] Gros and Steinherr (1995, 86).
[13] Gros and Steinherr (1995, 86).

Western countries whose oligarchic and inward-looing politico-institu-tional framework [had] not had the chance to be dynamited away."[14] By the mid-1990s, most CEE countries had liberalized prices and witnessed the collapse of intra-Comecon trading.[15] But with outdated technology, poorer quality commodities, few established marketing connections, and facing the protectionist policies of major powers, CEE manufacturers found it difficult, if not nearly impossible, to break into external markets. The comparison to Western Europe also neglected the important his-toric context of the post-1945 political and economic world—economic boom and Marshall Aid that overwhelmingly benefitted Western Euro-pean states, as well as infrastructure development and tariff protection for industries in those states. Nearly 90 percent of Marshall Aid was issued in grant form, yet only 10 percent of that aid was received by postcommu-nist European states.[16] Historians note that only Poland received signifi-cant support from Western allies in the form of debt cancellation to both public and private creditors and EU assistance with a preferential status for agricultural imports.[17] Jan Drahokoupil[18] writes that Hungary, on the other hand, possessed the world's highest per capita debt and was obli-gated to earmark revenue raised by privatizing state-owned corporations.

The Expansion of Liberal-Democratic Government

Beginning in the mid-1970s, a significant number of states around the globe, including Southern Europe, adopted parliamentary government.

---

[14] Gros and Steinherr (1995, 86).

[15] The Council for Mutual Economic Assistance (abbreviation COMECON, CMEA, or CAME) was an economic organization from 1949 to 1991 under the leadership of the Soviet Union. The organization was comprised of coun-tries of the Eastern Bloc along with a number of communist states around the world. The term is often extended to include bilateral relations among members, because in the system of socialist international economic relations, multilat-eral accords tended to be implemented through a set of more detailed, bilateral agreements.

[16] Outhwaite (2010, 92).

[17] Dale (2011, 11).

[18] Drahokoupil (2009, 102).

In terms of the Second and Third Worlds, John Walton and David Seddon identify three potential pragmatic explanations for these shifts.[19] First, democracy provides a relatively stable environment for business. Second, the neoliberal ideology noted above is promoted by international financial organizations and favors non-interventionist states. Liberal democratic governments fulfill this role because they "dilute state power to a level acceptable to diverse coalitions, just as they give greater power to the free play of markets."[20] Finally, debt and austerity can lead to "partial state breakdown," as the measures required by structural adjustment programs impede the ability of authoritarian governments to extend patronage and austerity policies require the support of large portions of the polity.

One of the major potential impediments to mature liberal democracy in the CEE countries during the early-1990s was the fact that independent and impartial political and civil institutions barely existed (with the exception of the Czech lands). As Robert Bideleux and Ian Jeffries[21] write:

> Even those [institutions] that did emerge had been largely destroyed by the combined effects of intolerant 'ethnic' nationalism and authoritarianism, the 1930s Great Depression, fascism, the Second World War, the Holocaust and neo-Stalinist dictatorship, all of which had helped to decimate, emasculate, or drive abroad the ethnic and social groups that were most capable of producing or recreating autonomous, pluralistic and liberal-minded 'civil societies.'

In other words, "No bourgeoisie, no democracy."[22] An example of this in the CEE context of transition is Poland in 1989. As General Jaruzelski noted, after initial steps toward democracy were taken "we tried economic reforms time and again. But we always met with public resistance and

---

[19] Walton and Seddon (1994, 334–35); Hoogvelt (1997); Derluguian (2005).
[20] Walton and Seddon (1994, 334–35); Hoogvelt (1997); Derluguian (2005).
[21] Bideleux and Jeffries (2007, 540–41).
[22] Moore (1969).

explosions. It is very different now. Now, with a government that enjoys public confidence, it has become possible to demand sacrifices."[23]

The Collapse of Labor and the Left

Another trend impacting the transition of CEE countries was the global downturn and the effect on the labor movement and social movements of the political Left. Control over industrial production shifted toward full-time officials, and as their industrial strength waned labor groups turned to leftist political parties for assistance. G.M. Tamás and Stuart Shields argue that both groups "accepted the present," defeat of their vision for political and economic life and the idealization of Western institutions that would shape the post-1989 global environment.[24] In parts of CEE, democratic reformers promoted a market-fundamentalist agenda, encouraged by Western foundations and governments.[25]

Post-Communist Economic Transformations

Economists and historians studying the transformations argue that it is misleading to label the post-communist economic transformations as moving from "socialism" to "capitalism."[26] Rather, they should be understood as movements from "state capitalism" to more liberalized and marketized versions of capitalism. Those changes involved major shifts from effectively "vertical" economic power structures to more "horizontal" relationships in which parties interacted more with one another than the state bureaucratic organization. The broad steps to shifting the economies in this direction included emphasizing (and sometimes introducing) the rule of law, encouraging stricter fiscal discipline, creating market institutions, encouraging greater competition and a more "level playing field," and investing in new infrastructure and technology, all while supporting privatization.

---

[23] Quoted in Haynes and Hasan (1998). See also Dale (2004, 274–75).
[24] Tamás (2011, 21–48); Shields (2011).
[25] Bandelj (2008, 115).
[26] See Sachs (1994); Sjöberg and Wyzan (1991); Taras (1992).

Essentially, the change from centrally planned command economies to more market-oriented economies required:

> not only proper macro-economic policies and institutions but also well-defined behavioral rules for integrating the decisions of decentralized agents... Perhaps of utmost importance is rule certainty for all economic agents.[27]

In each state, the initial challenge for the transition was stabilization. High hopes in late-1989 and the early-1990s were quickly deflated by realities of falling output, soaring inflation, rising unemployment, fiscal retrenchment, infrastructure decay, and simmering interethnic tensions, particularly in the Balkans and Slovakia. Many economists and politicians advocated mobilizing Western aid to the CEE states on a scale of the Marshall Plan and rejected the notion by skeptics contending that these countries were incapable of using it effectively. They argued that the CEE states could become Europe's "tiger economies," possessing substantial reserves of cheap, underemployed, skilled and educated labor with a "strong drive to prosper." Jeffrey Sachs, who served as an economic advisor to Poland between 1989 and 1991, argued:

> Western aid could help sustain political support for the reforms long enough for them to take hold. The Marshall Plan did not provide Europe with the funds for economic recovery. It provided governments with enough financial backing to achieve economic and political stability give hope to the population and thus make economic recovery possible.[28]

Economists, such as Sachs, warned that if the West failed to provide short-term assistance it would be faced with the choice of having to "do business" with lack-luster states and economies rife with corruption.

---

[27] van Brabant (1989).
[28] *International Herald Tribune.* May 16, 1991. New York, NY: New York Times Company. Microfilm. Clark University Library.

Western states did not provide large-scale grants of aid, however, and CEE states felt the impact of this almost immediately in their attempts to recover from the early 1990s economic collapse. According to reports by economic historians and global institutions, such as the World Bank, the collapse of traditional trade and investment links and dislocation of domestic demand contributed to large output collapses in the early years of transition, ranging from about 10 percent in Poland and Hungary to some 40 percent in countries such as Latvia and Lithuania. As prices were liberalized, they tended to skyrocket, partly as relative prices were set by supply and demand rather than central planning, but with especially steep increases where state revenues dried up and governments had few sources of finance other than turning to central banks to print money. In 1994, the United Nations Children's Fund (UNICEF) released a report claiming the collapse of European command economies had precipitated a slump in birth rates and major increases in poverty, death rates, morbidity rates, malnutrition, truancy, family breakdown, and violent crime. The result was such that by 1993 conditions in the eastern half of the European continents were worse than those in Latin America during the "lost decade" of the 1980s or in Western Europe during the 1930s depression.[29]

According to Bideleux and Jeffries, partially reconstructed ex-communist organizations continued to operate in Romania until 1996, Slovakia and Bulgaria until 1998, Croatia until 1999, and Serbia until 2000. Similar problems were evident in Poland and Hungary, while large sectors of the economies of Serbia, Montenegro, Bulgaria, Macedonia, Bosnia, and Albania fell under the control of "organized criminal networks, blackmarketeers, armed thugs, and traffickers in fuel, drugs, arms, cigarettes, and prostitutes."[30]

In many ways the post-1989 political and economic transformations of the CEE countries were even more fraught with difficulties than the post-1918 and post-1945 efforts. Although the Balkan and CEE economies suffered severe human losses, war damage, and dislocation in both of the prior postwar periods, they were comparably less industrialized than

---

[29] *The Independent* (1994, 10).
[30] Bideleux and Jeffries (2007, 551).

in 1989 and did not have to contend with "extensive closures of industrial capacity."[31] Historians note that even if they were subject to wartime controls, they were still already market economies. This prevented them from undergoing simultaneous economic reconstruction, stabilization programs, and the profound reordering of their economic systems.

When CEE countries began their post-1989 transformations, most of them were already burdened with large foreign debts (see Table 1.1) and heavy debt-service payments inherited from the outgoing communist regimes. In 1918 and 1945, they had the opportunity to begin their new states with relatively clean slates.

Despite the many challenges outlined in the 1994 UNICEF report, the CEE post-communist states, with the exceptions of Bosnia and Macedonia, were achieving significant economic growth. Their efforts to establish market economies were more or less effective, again with the exception of Bosnia. As discussed in more detail in the subsequent country case studies, the initially high levels of inflation were largely brought under control through monetary policy by most CEE states in 1993, in Latvia and Albania by 1994, in Estonia, Romania, Croatia, Bosnia, and Macedonia in 1995, in Lithuania by 1996, and Serbia-Montenegro and Bulgaria by 1998.

Even with measurable progress in the 1990s, the figures presented in the tables below illustrate the significance of the technical and economic

Table 1.1 *Hard-currency debts of European communist states, 1979 ($)*

	Total ($ billion)	$ per inhabitant
Yugoslavia	17	780
Hungary	7.5	700
Poland	19.5	557
Romania	7	320
Bulgaria	4	455
Czechoslovakia	3.5	233
USSR	10.2	39

Source: Bideleux (1987, 270).

---

[31] Bideleux and Jeffries (2007, 554).

Table 1.2 Cars, personal computers, and computer linked to Internet per 100 inhabitants (1999–2000)

	Cars	PCs	PCs linked to Internet
EU-15 average	46.1	24.8	2.3
Slovenia	42.6	25.3	1.2
Estonia	33.9	13.5	2.1
Czech Republic	36.2	10.7	1.2
Latvia	23.5	8.2	0.8
Hungary	23.5	7.4	1.2
Slovakia	23.6	7.4	0.5
Poland	25.9	6.2	0.4
Lithuania	31.7	5.9	0.4
Bulgaria	24.4	2.7	0.2
Romania	13.9	2.7	0.2

Source: European Commission. December 13, 2003. Press Release, State/01/129, p. 4.

gap between the EU-15 and CEE states.[32] Table 1.2 presents data on the numbers of cars, personal computers, and computers connected to the Internet per 100 inhabitants as of 1999.

Table 1.3 provides figures on the percentage of the workforce employed in "knowledge-intensive services" and tech manufacturing. Finally, the data on disparities in hourly labor costs between the EU-15 states and the accession states, as depicted in Table 1.4, reveals the extent of the gap between the two regions in a way not fully captured by other studies utilizing per capita GDP.

Foreign Direct Investment

Foreign direct investment (FDI) entails investing directly in production in another country, either by buying a company there or establishing new operations of an existing business. This is done mostly by companies as

---

[32] The EU-15 is composed of Austria, Belgium, Denmark, Finland, France, Germany, Greece, Ireland, Italy, Luxembourg, the Netherlands, Portugal, Spain, Sweden, and the United Kingdom.

Table 1.3 Percentage of workforce employment in knowledge-intensive services and medium- and high-tech manufacturing (2002)

	Knowledge-intensive services	Medium- and high-tech manufacturing
EU-15 average	33.3	7.4
Estonia	30.9	3.4
Hungary	26.4	8.5
Lithuania	24.7	2.6
Latvia	24.7	1.9
Slovakia	24.0	8.2
Czech Republic	23.9	8.9
Slovenia	22.8	9.2
Bulgaria	22.2	5.3
Romania	12.8	5.5

Source: European Commission. November 7, 2003. Press Release, STAT/03/127, pp. 1–2. No data available for Poland.

Table 1.4 Hourly labor costs in industry and services (2000)[33]

EU-15 average[34]	22.70	Accession states' average	4.21
Sweden	28.56	Cyprus	10.74
Denmark	27.10	Slovenia	8.98
Germany	26.54	Poland	4.48
France	24.39	Czech Republic	3.90
United Kingdom	23.85	Hungary	3.83
Austria	23.60	Slovakia	3.06
Netherlands	22.99	Estonia	3.03
Ireland	17.34	Lithuania	2.71
Spain	14.22	Latvia	2.42
Greece	10.40	Romania	1.51
Portugal	8.13	Bulgaria	1.35

Source: EU Press Release. March 3, 2003. STAT/03/23, p. 2.

---

[33] Note: The average hourly labor costs are total annual labor costs divided by the total number of hours worked during the year.

[34] Excluding Italy and Belgium, no available data.

opposed to financial institutions, which prefer indirect investment abroad such as buying small parcels of a country's supply of shares or bonds. FDI grew rapidly during the 1990s before slowing a bit, along with the global economy, in the early years of the 21st century. Most of this investment went from one member-country of the Organization for Economic Cooperation and Development (OECD) to another, but the share going to developing countries, especially in Asia, increased steadily.[35]

There was a time when economists considered FDI a substitute for trade. Building factories in foreign countries was one way of jumping tariff barriers. Now economists typically regard FDI and trade as complementary. For example, a firm can use a factory in one country to supply neighboring markets. Some investments, especially in services industries, are essential prerequisites for selling to foreigners. Who would buy a Whopper in London if it had to be sent from Chicago?

Governments used to be highly suspicious of FDI, often regarding it as corporate imperialism. Nowadays they are more likely to court it. They hope that investors will create jobs, and bring expertise and technology that will be passed on to local firms and workers, helping to sharpen up their whole economy. Furthermore, unlike financial investors, multinationals generally invest directly in plant and equipment. Since it is hard to uproot a chemical factory, these investments, once made, are far more enduring than the flows of money that whisk in and out of emerging markets.

Although FDI was restricted before 1989, foreign investors started entering the region after the fall of the communist regimes and it has been considered particularly important to CEE economies.[36] Economists and international financial organizations have cited FDI as "an engine for transition" to a market-based economy and a "powerful force for integration"

---

[35] For more information on studying foreign direct investment (FDI), see www.economist.com/economics-a-to-z#2DI6CRzKPkRSqArm.99

[36] Along with efforts to reform their socialist regimes, Hungary, Poland, and Yugoslavia allowed joint ventures with foreign investors prior to 1989. The provisions, however, only really began to see the effects of FDI beginning in 1989, as demonstrated by the data in Table 1.5, "Foreign Direct Investment Trends."

of this region into the larger global economy.[37] Absent "massive inflows of foreign capital," they believed "successful transition [from planned to market economies] in CEE is unlikely."[38] Many believed that FDI would prove to be the catalyst in a transition away from socialist economies and positively affect macroeconomic indicators such as balance of payment and unemployment. Foreign investors would introduce technological and managerial resources, along with financial capital, and encourage corporate restructuring and privatization of state-owned firms.[39]

As Table 1.5 shows, the initial FDI inflows were minimal, but rapidly grew after 1995. Between 1995 and 2004, average FDI stock as percent share in GDP for CEE countries has been higher than the world average. By 2004, it was almost twice as high, contributing on average to 39 percent GDP. This placed the CEE among the world's top regions in terms of foreign capital penetration at that time.[40]

Although these inflows formed a significant portion of the CEE economy, for the entire CEE region, FDI between 1989 and 1994 amounted to only two-fifths of the flow to China in 1993 alone. These differences in regional FDI are partially explained by differences in investor countries to both regions. As displayed in Table 1.6, the primary regional investors in the CEE countries during the transition were not identical to the top worldwide investors.

Germany and the Netherlands rank higher than the United States based on total stock of investment in the region as of 2000, while France and the United Kingdom had a much less significant presence. Austria and Sweden, although ranked 23rd and 13th, respectively, were much more prominent investors.

---

[37] IMF (1997); UNCTAD (1998).

[38] Schmidt (1995).

[39] Meyer (1995, 1998); Lankes and Venables (1996); OECD (1998); Bevin and Estrin (2004).

[40] According to the UNCTAD (2006), data for the period revealed only one other region higher in FDI stock as percent of GDP, "Developing America, other." This category by their definition included island states of Central America where FDI stock as percent of GDP was 43.

Table 1.5 Foreign direct investment trends during the transition (1970–2004)

	FDI Inflows ($ billion)		Average FDI Stock as % GDP	
	CEE	**World**	**CEE**	**World**
1970	0	13	0	-
1980	0	55	0	5
1989	<1	193	0	8
1990	<1	208	0	8
1991	2	161	2	8
1992	3	169	5	8
1993	4	228	7	9
1994	4	259	9	9
1995	10	341	10	9
1996	9	393	12	10
1997	10	488	16	12
1998	18	701	19	14
1999	19	1092	23	16
2000	21	1397	27	18
2001	22	826	31	20
2002	25	716	35	21
2003	17	633	37	22
2004	28	648	39	22

Note: CEE in this table includes Bulgaria, Croatia, Czech Republic, Estonia, Hungary, Latvia, Lithuania, Poland, Romania, Slovakia, and Slovenia.

Source: UNCTAD (2006).[41]

Table 1.6 Top Investor Countries in 2000

	World	**CEE**
1.	United States	Germany
2.	United Kingdom	Netherlands (#7 in the world)
3.	France	United States
4.	Germany	Austria (#23 in the world)
5.	Hong Kong	Sweden (#13 in the world)

Note: Rankings are based on outward FDI stock as of 2000.
Source: UNCTAD (2001).

[41] http://unctadstat.unctad.org/EN/Index.html

These relationships are further complicated when one examines the presence of significant worldwide investors in individual CEE countries during the transition. Table 1.7 highlights these disparities in percent share of total FDI stock across the CEE region nearly 10 years after the fall of the communist regimes. The Czech Republic and Poland received the greatest share of investment to CEE states. German corporations were heavily invested throughout the central part of Europe, (Czech Republic, Hungary, Poland, Romania, and Slovakia) more so than the Baltic states of Estonia, Latvia, and Lithuania. Comparing the latter, Estonia received the greatest investment from Finland, while Denmark and Sweden invested in Lithuania and Latvia. In 2000, the United States investment amounted to nearly 20 percent of FDI stock in Croatia, but less than 5 percent in nearby Slovenia. Investments by Latin American, South African, and Asia countries were negligible across the region.

How do we explain the difference in investment patterns across the region? Scholars writing in economic sociology argue that the pre-existing social and cultural relationships shared across these regions facilitated these economic patterns.[42] Nina Bandelj writes:

> In cases where uncertainty surrounding economic transactions is high, such as in post-communist Europe during the transition period, the role of social relations and pre-existing knowledge of potential partners in facilitating FDI transactions is even more pronounced.[43]

Bandelj argues that scholars can trace the inflows of FDI to pre-existing international relations and cultural affinities between investor and recipient countries, even when measured against geographic proximity.[44]

Despite the optimism surrounding the power of FDI by economic advisors, when examining the transition period between 1990 and 2010 as a whole, economic data reveals that a significant portion of the CEE

---

[42] Smith and Powell (2005, 379–402).

[43] Bandelj (2007, 45).

[44] Bandelj (2008).

Table 1.7 Investments by significant worldwide investor countries in CEE (% share of total FDI stock in host in 2000)

World Ranking	Investor Country	Bulgaria	Croatia	Czech Republic	Estonia	Hungary	Latvia	Lithuania	Poland	Slovakia	Slovenia
1	US	12	21	6	5	8	9	10	10	7	4
2	UK	11	2	3	2	1	5	7	3	3	4
3	France	3	2	4	1	7	<1	1	12	3	11
4	Germany	19	22	26	3	26	11	7	19	28	12
5	Hong Kong	0	0	0	<1	0	1	<1	<1	0	<1
6	Belgium/ Luxembourg	6	6	5	<1	5	<1	4	2	2	<1
7	Netherlands	4	4	30	2	23	3	1	25	24	3
8	Japan	<1	0	<1	<1	2	0	<1	<1	0	<1
9	Switzerland	3	1	4	1	2	2	5	2	<1	4
10	Canada	<1	<1	<1	<1	<1	<1	<1	<1	<1	<1
11	Italy	2	2	<1	<1	3	<1	<1	4	2	5
12	Spain	3	<1	<1	<1	<1	<1	<1	2	<1	0
13	Sweden	<1	2	<11	40	<1	13	17	3	<1	<1
14	Australia	<1	1	<1	0	0	0	<1	<1	0	<1
15	Singapore	<1	0	0	1	<1	1	0	<1	0	<1

(Continued)

Table 1.7 Investments by significant worldwide investor countries in CEE (% share of total FDI stock in host in 2000) (Continued)

World Ranking	Investor Country	Bulgaria	Croatia	Czech Republic	Estonia	Hungary	Latvia	Lithuania	Poland	Slovakia	Slovenia
16	Finland	<1	<1	<1	30	<1	6	6	<1	<1	<1
17	Taiwan	0	0	<1	0	0	0	0	<1	0	0
18	Denmark	<1	<1	1	4	<1	10	18	2	<1	1
19	Norway	<1	<1	<1	4	<1	6	4	<1	<1	0
20	South Africa	0	0	0	0	0	0	0	<1	0	0
21	China	<1	0	<1	<1	<1	0	<1	<1	0	0
22	South Korea	<1	0	<1	0	<1	<1	<1	<1	0	0
23	Austria	6	25	11	<1	12	<1	<1	3	14	46
24	Argentina	0	0	0	0	0	0	0	<1	0	0
25	Malaysia	0	0	<1	0	0	0	0	0	0	0

Source: UNCTAD (2001, 2006), percentages tabulated manually.

region experienced a regional Great Depression. Currencies across the region devalued rapidly and banking crises were widespread. In terms of GDP, nearly two decades were lost.[45] In some cases, where there was adequate political and institutional support for fiscal and monetary discipline, stabilization was achieved within a couple of years; others faced longer or multiple attempts to establish low inflation and sustainable public finances.

Following a period of stabilization, the new member states focused on institution building to improve the functioning of the economies, using Western Europe and other democratic states as models. Many of these countries, however, faced significant challenges in privatization, public sector reform, and establishment of an environment conducive to reform. Scholars credit the creation of credible monetary and exchange rate frameworks—whether involving floating or different types of fixed-rate arrangements—as key to the success of transition. Reza Moghadam, Director of the International Monetary Fund (IMF's) European Department, argues, "integration has been particularly evident in the financial sector, with western European banks dominating in most of the transition countries."[46] This relationship has had both positive and negative consequences for transitioning states. On the one hand, it brought critical expertise in financing; on the other hand, the unrestricted flow of capital into the region in the early to mid-2000s inflated bubbles that burst in the ensuing global financial crisis.

Many experts take the position that integration has also contributed to strong convergence of incomes. Average GDP per capita across emerging Europe relative to advanced economies in Europe rose by about 50 percent between 1995 and 2013, despite the recent crisis. Sizable trade and investment links with Western Europe were key to the growth and convergence progress that brought emerging Europe's income levels nearly half the levels of their advanced economy neighbors.

---

[45] Dale (2011, 11).

[46] www.imf.org/external/pubs/ft/fandd/2014/03/moghadam.htm

Conclusion

The CEE states experienced several significant periods of transition in the 20th century, marked by the events of 1918, 1945, and 1989. In both 1918 and 1945, the CEE and Balkan economies were suffering from devastating losses, destruction, and dislocation. Although they needed to focus on economic restructuring and stabilization, they did not have to profoundly reinvent their economic and political systems. The post-1989 transformations, however, were complicated by large foreign debts and debt-service payments inherited from the outgoing communist regimes. They were not in the process of recovering from a World War, but did struggle to recover from a state of economic collapse, high levels of inflation, severe infrastructure neglect and decay, environmental crises, the political anxieties of the Cold War, and in some cases, internal ethnic conflict.

The next chapter will proceed with an analysis of the role of the EU and economic integration in CEE economies, followed by a discussion of current market trends in each of the regional blocks in Chapter 3. Chapter 4 examines the integration of East and West through the establishment of supply chains and manufacturing satellites in the region, while Chapter 5 will assess the economic impact of the recent global economic crises on the CEE economies. Finally, the text will conclude with a discussion of the challenges and divergence among the CEE, Southeastern Europe (SEE), and Commonwealth of Independent State (CIS) countries, including individual case studies analyzing political risk within each state.

CHAPTER 2

The Role of the European Union in Eastern European Economies

Historians, economists, and political scientists have described the transition process following the post-1989 collapse of communist regimes throughout the Central and Eastern European (CEE) states as a "return to Europe."[1] The task of "reconnecting" with Europe reflected a desire on the part of the elites and a significant portion of the public in these states to (re)claim a heritage or identity that, in political terms, entailed the creation of liberal democratic institutions and, in economic terms, a move toward the creation of market economies. Many believed this would be achieved gradually through participation in European integration and a single market. This chapter will provide the reader with information on the gradual integration of the CEE post-communist states into the European Union (EU) since the mid-1990s—as well as the ways in which this process interacted with the political and economic transformations taking place in those regions.

Accession, Negotiation, and the EU

By May 2007, most CEE states had become member states of the EU leaving only the Western Balkans and several former-Soviet Union states outside the EU. In outlining the process for EU accession, the Treaty on the EU states that any European country may apply for membership if it respects the democratic values of the EU and is committed to

---

[1] For just a few examples of the use of "return to Europe," see: Alan Smith (2000); Bideleux and Jeffries (2007); Wolchik and Curry (2011); Jacoby (2004).

promoting them. The country must meet the key criteria for accession, as defined at the European Council in Copenhagen in 1993 and referred to as "Copenhagen criteria."[2] The criteria, in essence, state that countries need to possess: (1) stable institutions guaranteeing democracy, the rule of law, human rights, and respect for and protection of minorities; (2) a functioning market economy and the capacity to cope with competition and market forces in the EU; and (3) the ability to take on and implement effectively the obligations of membership, including adherence to the aims of political, economic and monetary union.[3] The process for states proceeds in three steps:

1. When a country is ready, it becomes an official candidate for membership—but this does not necessarily mean that formal negotiations have been opened.
2. The candidate moves on to formal membership negotiations, a process that involves the adoption of established EU law, preparations to be in a position to properly apply and enforce it and implementation of judicial, administrative, economic, and other reforms necessary for the country to meet the conditions for joining, known as accession criteria.
3. When the negotiations and accompanying reforms have been completed to the satisfaction of both sides, the country can join the EU.[4]

Some elements of the process of accession are subject to negotiation, such as *financial arrangements*—how much the new member is likely to pay into and receive from the EU budget (in the form of transfers) or *transitional arrangements*—sometimes certain rules are phased in gradually, to give the new or existing members time to adapt.[5]

The elements of this process are reflected in the series of transitions experienced by the EU in the 20th century. Historians of the EU mark

[2] See the European Commission (1993).
[3] European Commission (2015).
[4] European Commission (n.d.).
[5] European Commission (2015).

the decade of the 1990s for Europe as one "without frontiers."[6] The signing of the Single European Act of 1986, which provided the basis for a 6-year program aimed at liberalizing free trade across the EU borders in a single market, was completed with the adoption of the "four freedoms" in 1993, the movement of goods, services, people, and money. The formation of the single market was also complemented by the creation of the "Maastricht" Treaty on EU in 1993 and the Treaty of Amsterdam in 1999.

The Maastricht Treaty and the Euro

Europe's core countries continued to grow closer in the transition and accession processes. In the early stages, exchange rate variability between member states was reduced through the European Exchange Rate Mechanism (ERM), which allowed currencies to fluctuate around parities within predefined bands. In 1990, exchange controls within the European Economic Community were abolished, allowing for the free flow of capital. Although there were crises under the ERM—for example, the United Kingdom was forced out in 1992 when the value of the pound sterling fell below ERM limits—realignments became less frequent over time as monetary policies and inflation rates converged.[7]

The idea of a common currency slowly gained traction, but it was not until the Maastricht Treaty of 1992 that the "Economic and Monetary Union," and with it a common currency and monetary policy, truly began to take shape. While creation of a single currency was rooted in Europe's integration and facilitating economic transactions within the union, it also helped place the unified Germany that emerged at the end of the Cold War solidly within a common European institutional framework.[8]

The Maastricht Treaty established convergence criteria to ensure that countries joining the new common currency would be sufficiently similar, and it also gave market forces a significant role in disciplining member

---

[6] European Commission (2015).
[7] ERM Exchange Rate Method (2001).
[8] Treaty of Maastricht on European Union (n.d.).

states, by establishing the "no bailout" clause.[9] To dispel skepticism and preserve fiscal discipline after the common currency was introduced, member countries signed the Stability and Growth Pact in 1997, which was designed to tie policies to fiscal balance and debt targets.[10]

During the initial stages of CEE accession, external economic assistance came mainly from other countries and international institutions such as the International Monetary Fund (IMF), the World Bank, and the new European Bank for Reconstruction and Development. But as the process of accession gained steam, the EU became a critical force in developing institutions, guiding economic policy, and financing infrastructure for the transitioning states. The process culminated in EU accession for 11 countries (4 of them already euro-area members), and candidate status for an additional three. Reza Moghadam and others argue that this achievement was "inconceivable" 24 years prior and brought tremendous benefits both to the transition countries and to the existing EU members through increased trade, capital, and labor flows.

The Complexities of Accession for CEE States

The path to EU membership, however, was longer and more complex for the CEE states than many of those in neighboring regions (Southern Europe, for example).[11] The CEE states varied significantly in their preparedness for EU membership and with respect to the "political effort" they were willing to undertake to reform their institutions and move closer to accession.[12] EU accession was a broadly, not universally, shared aspiration, as evidenced by the domestic political, social, and economic debates that emerged within the CEE states. Parties who feared themselves "transition losers" included workers in state-subsidized heavy industries, the public sector, small farmers, and individuals on fixed incomes. Social groups emerged with objections to accession on religious, cultural, or ideological

---

[9] Treaty of Maastricht on European Union (n.d.).

[10] Resolution of the European Council on the Stability and Growth Pact Amsterdam (1997).

[11] Heinisch and Landsberger (n.d.).

[12] Heinisch and Landsberger (n.d.).

grounds. Some parties within the CEE states expressed concerns about the general transition to a market economy and the impact of globalization, political corruption, or bureaucratic incompetence, expressing fears that extended beyond accession. After the collapse of communism, CEE countries found themselves in a potential security vacuum and feared the possibility of returning to totalitarianism, secessionist movements, nationalist movements, or paralyzing political fragmentation that could jeopardize their potential future security, stability, and economic growth. This led to a push for "quick accession to the EU...to ensure this region remained on the path of growth."[13]

With the opening of accession negotiations, public debate shifted; the public and political elites became more aware of possible consequences of accession and the debate moved from generalities to specifics.[14] Further, the exclusion of the CEE states from the European integration process until their official membership in 2004 and 2007, and the long accession negotiation periods undermined the initially strong enthusiasm among the public.[15] What began as a "euroenthusiastic" process of accession and the "return to Europe," quickly transitioned to "euroscepticism," and a realization of the complexity of reform measures that needed adoption.[16] Cecile Leconte and others argue that in countries where such processes are lengthy and drawn-out, the "perception of a link between the processes can be eroded."[17]

Nonetheless, the CEE countries adopted some form of economic liberalization, including changes to monetary policy, elimination of hyperinflation, independence of the Central Banks, and unification of exchange rates.[18] The reforms and EU accession led to positive social, economic, and political benefits for most of the CEE states. Broadly speaking, the EU enlargement to include CEE states provided the "needed impetus

---

[13]   de Crombruggle, Minton-Beddoes, and Sachs (1996, 3).
[14]   Whitefield and Rohrschneider (2006).
[15]   Medrano (2003).
[16]   Taggart (1998).
[17]   Leconte (2010).
[18]   Tupy (2003).

for their political and economic modernization."[19] It united Europe in a common vision of democracy, stability, prosperity, and a growing internal market with over 500 million people. For this reason, the 2004 and 2007 enlargements were unique "due to the number of acceding countries, their size, their comparatively low levels of economic development, the predominance of their agrarian sector, and their post-communist past."[20]

Security Considerations

The enlargement, in many ways, complemented the North Atlantic Treaty Organization (NATO) in "filling the security vacuum resulting from the dismantling of the Soviet empire."[21] Following the signing of the Balladue Pact in 1993, the EU could help diffuse threats posed by the collapse of communism or any border disputes. In the case of Poland and Romania, for example, "the EU could minimize the inflow of migrants, drugs, arms, and human trafficking" which constituted important security concerns for both states in the post-communist transition period.[22]

Economic Considerations

CEE accession to the EU opened the way for people to freely travel across national boundaries, reconnect with friends and family in other states, and more easily relocate to other member states, if desired. With the support of the Erasmus Programme, students from CEE countries could complete their education at Western universities and the possibility of study abroad was viewed positively by nearly 84 percent of EU citizens.[23] In the case of Romania, for example, university students and faculty received scholarships to study at Western EU member states to address a chronic shortage of investment in education and research in the Romania state.[24] This was

---

[19] Serbos (2008).

[20] Faber (2009, 21).

[21] Stoian (2005, 12).

[22] Stoian (2005, 13).

[23] BIS: Department of Business, Innovation, and Skills (2010).

[24] Guyader (2009, 102).

not an isolated case. According to a report produced by the European Commission in 2010, more than 15 million citizens have moved to other EU countries to work or enjoy retirement, benefitting from social benefit transferability and the enlargement of the Schengen Area.[25]

These positive social changes also illustrate the strength of the EU as an economic unit. The EU is one of the strongest and largest economic, free trade areas in the world. As noted previously, the Treaty of Rome of 1957 based Europe's reconstruction on the gradual development of a borderless common market involving the free movement of goods, services, people, and capital between participating countries.[26] This early vision evolved into the European Monetary System, a precursor to the economic and monetary union launched in 1979, and the 1992 Maastricht Treaty, establishing the European Central Bank.

Despite the rises and falls of the transition period for most CEE states, the process of economic reform and accession led to strong convergence with the western side of Europe. Even before they achieved full members, Poland, the Czech Republic, and Hungary experienced strong initial growth in GDP.[27] In Poland, between May and August 2007, economic growth was nearly 6.5 percent and unemployment declined from 20 percent (2003) to nearly 11.4 percent.[28] In Hungary, imports from other new member states increased from €4 billion in 2003 to €13.7 billion by 2007.[29] After EU accession, a wider financial market in Slovenia opened access to capital that stimulated import-export activity across small, medium, and large enterprises.[30] FDI sharply increased in Bulgaria, as well as GDP—which grew from nearly 35 million BGN (Bulgarian Lev) in 2003 to nearly 57 million BGN in 2007.[31] On average, income per capita rose from about 30 percent of EU15 levels in the mid-1990s to

---

[25] BIS: Department of Business, Innovation, and Skills (2010).

[26] For more information, see: *The European Union Explained: Economic and Monetary Union and the euro* (2014).

[27] BIS: Department of Business, Innovation, and Skills (2010).

[28] Karasinka-Fendler (2009).

[29] Szemler (2009).

[30] Kajne (2009).

[31] Krassimir and Kaloyan (2009).

around 50 percent in 2014.[32] That average, noted in a 2014 IMF Report, does not include the difference between CEE countries, with some states, such as the Baltics, making huge advances; and others, such as Bosnia and Herzegovina, Moldova, and Ukraine, getting increasingly left behind. On the whole, however, price levels and wages have risen as part of the convergence process.

Political Considerations

In addition to incentives for growth and economic reform, accession to the EU required substantial political reforms in CEE countries. The EU standards imposed criteria for democratization that "aimed at minimizing the danger of a return to authoritarian regimes and centrally planned economies."[33] Following the guidelines of the Copenhagen Criteria and the adoption of the EU *acquis*, most CEE countries underwent extensive political reform between 1992 and 2002. Many adopted a parliamentary system of government similar to states in Western Europe, as opposed to the presidential system favored by members of the former Soviet bloc.[34] Since that time, most states consciously adopt reforms that bring their governing institutions in closer alignment with western liberal democracies. In Poland, for example, the state's commitment to EU accession led to changes in the Polish constitution, which diminished the ability for an authoritarian regime to emerge. In Romania, the 1996 election of the Romanian Democratic Convention removed communists from power. This is not to say that politics and institutions are perfectly aligned in the CEE states, and this will be discussed in more detail in Chapter 6, "Political Risk in Eastern Europe."

The Adoption of the Euro

Before the adoption of the euro and the post-communist transition, CEE states experienced price distortions, with prices detached from market

---

[32] Roaf et al. (2014, 5).

[33] Stoian (2005, 8).

[34] For more on this, see Beachain, Sheridan, and Stan (2012).

forces. Trading took place primarily among Comecon members, with limited trade with the rest of the world. To integrate the post-communist economies into the international monetary and trading systems, several reforms were needed: liberalization of prices, establishment of currencies as units of exchange, and the establishment of functioning, autonomous, accountable central banks.

CEE states varied widely in their experiences with these reforms. For example, Poland's new central bank law in 1989 established the independence of the governor, distributed previous commercial banking activities to nine commercial banks, and set a central goal of "strengthening of the Polish currency." Czechoslovakia adopted similar reforms in 1990. Countries that were not able to adopt these types of reforms (i.e., Bulgaria, Romania, Russia, and Ukraine) were forced to undergo more than one round of stabilization.

For CEE countries, multiple rounds of accession, negotiation, and reform also mark membership in the EU. The euro area includes those EU member states that have adopted the single currency. But the euro area is not static–under the Treaty on the European Union (Maastricht Treaty), all EU member states have to join the euro area once the necessary conditions are fulfilled, except Denmark and the United Kingdom, which have negotiated an "opt-out" clause that allows them to remain outside the euro area.[35]

CEE accession countries that plan to join the EU must align many aspects of its society—social, economic, and political—with those of other western EU member states. According to the European Commission, the purpose of this alignment is to ensure that an accession country can operate successfully within the EU's single market for goods, services, capital, and labor—accession is a process of integration.

In this structure, adopting the euro and joining the euro area takes integration to a step further—"it is a process of much closer economic integration with the other euro-area member states."[36] Adopting the euro is an exhaustive process that requires even greater economic and legal convergence.

---

[35] "Economic and Financial Affairs: Adopting the Euro" (n.d.).

[36] European Commission (n.d.).

The euro's architecture was built on the premise that market forces, combined with minimal coordination of policies, would sufficiently align economies, discipline fiscal policies, and allow countries to withstand idiosyncratic shocks. According to Susan Schadler and other scholars, "relinquishing monetary policy could lead to greater economic volatility unless adjustment to shocks that are asymmetric with respect to the euro area occurs efficiently through other channels—primarily fiscal policy and wage and price flexibility—or the incidence of such shocks is reduced owing to the discipline of the euro-area macroeconomic policy framework and the elimination of variable emerging market risk premia."[37] At the time of Schadler's study, economists identified the Baltic states— Estonia, Latvia, and Lithuania—as having closer policy links with the euro area, while five other central European countries—the Czech Republic, Hungary, Poland, the Slovak Republic, and Slovenia—as requiring major changes in their macroeconomic policies and policy frameworks in their efforts toward adoption of the euro.

In October 2004, the European Commission chose to assess the 10 countries joining the EU. Although the maximum 2-year period referred to by the Treaty had not yet elapsed for these countries in 2004, the obligatory reassessment of Sweden was taken as an opportunity to analyze also the state of convergence in the new member states. The report concluded that none of the 11 assessed countries at that stage fulfilled the necessary conditions for the adoption of the single currency.[38]

Since that time, multiple assessments of the CEE states have taken place. In 2013, the European Commission finally concluded that Latvia fulfilled all conditions for adopting the euro, and in 2014 they came to a similar conclusion regarding Lithuania. The next regular convergence assessment, covering all member states with derogation, is scheduled for June 2016.

Given the incredibly stringent rules and multiple layers of assessment, as well as the extended timetable for adoption, one might wonder what possesses the CEE states (and other EU member states) to seek membership in the euro area. The European Commission cites the following

---

[37] Schadler et al. (2005, 1).

[38] European Commission (n.d.).

benefits: "more choice and stable prices for consumers and citizens; greater security and more opportunities for businesses and markets; improved economic stability and growth; more integrated financial markets; a stronger presence for the EU in the global economy; a tangible sign of a European identity."

Less optimistically, Ott Ummelas argues, "Euro membership proved that a country had the discipline to join one of the world's most exclusive clubs."[39] On May 20, 2011 Poland's central bank governor, Marek Belka, said his country and the region would not get the benefits they had anticipated from a quick adoption of the euro. As far back as December 2010, Czech Prime Minister Petr Necas said his country could refuse to adopt the single currency as long as it deems it beneficial to keep the koruna.

Yet, other CEE states have expressed a strong desire to join the euro area, or are glad they already took steps to do so. Hungarian Foreign Minister János Martonyi said on June 22, 2011 that adoption remained a primary goal. Slovenia, already a member, has profited from being inside such a large currency zone. Estonia, Latvia's and Lithuania's neighbor endured many hardships to join.[40] On balance, Harvard professor Jeffrey Frankel argues that monetary unions, such as the euro, facilitate trade. As trade patterns and cyclical correlations gradually shift toward Western Europe, the argument for euro adoption in the CEE states strengthens.[41]

---

[39] Ummelas (2011).

[40] Ummelas (2011).

[41] Frankel (2008).

CHAPTER 3

Central and Eastern European Economies

Introduction

As discussed in earlier chapters, the Central and Eastern Europe (CEE)[1] bloc is a generic term that defines the group of countries in central, southeast, northern, and eastern Europe, commonly meaning former communist states in Europe. It is in use since the collapse of the Iron Curtain[2] in 1989 to 1990, when more than 20 nations emerged from the isolation that had largely hidden them, and their citizens, from the rest of the world for more than 4 decades. As argued by Lerman, Csaki, and Feder (2004), in each of these former Soviet States, remnants of tradition and economic organization have prevented them from stepping out, beyond the curtain and onto the world stage. Nonetheless, some have been extremely successful.

The CEE bloc of countries includes all the Eastern Bloc countries west of the post-World War II border with the former Soviet Union. The Eastern Bloc was the name used by North Atlantic Treaty Organization (NATO)-affiliated countries for the former communist states of CEE, which generally included the Soviet Union and the countries of the Warsaw Pact.[3] The terms Communist Bloc and Soviet Bloc were also used

---

[1] In scholarly literature the abbreviations CEE or CEEC are often used for this concept.

[2] The notional barrier separating the former Soviet bloc and the West prior to the decline of communism that followed the political events in Eastern Europe in 1989.

[3] The Warsaw Pact, formally known as the Treaty of Friendship, Co-operation, and Mutual Assistance, and informally as WarPac, was a collective defense treaty among Soviet Union and seven Soviet satellite states in Central and Eastern Europe in existence during the Cold War; Hirsch, Kett, and Trefil (2002).

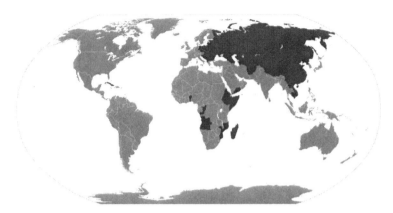

Figure 3.1 Countries that declared to be socialist and communist between 1979 and 1983

Source: Busky (2000).

to denote groupings of states aligned with the Soviet Union, although these terms might include states outside CEE. Figure 3.1 depicts a map of countries that declared themselves to be socialist states under the Marxist–Leninist or Maoist definition, in other words communist states, between 1979 and 1983. This period marked the greatest territorial extent of communist states.[4]

In addition, the CEE Bloc also includes the independent states in former Yugoslavia, which actually were not considered part of the Eastern Bloc, and the three Baltic States—Estonia, Latvia, and Lithuania, which chose not to join the Commonwealth of Independent States (CIS) with the other 12 former republics of the former Union of Soviet Socialist Republics (USSR).[5]

Recently, during the summer 2015, the Russian government publicly stated to the world that the Soviet government who gave away the Baltics was illegitimate and its decisions were illegal. Russia's Prosecutor General's Office launched at the time an improbable but nonetheless serious

---

[4] Busky (2000, 9).
[5] A former communist country in Eastern Europe and northern Asia; established in 1922; included Russia and 14 other soviet socialist republics (Ukraine and Byelorussia and others); officially dissolved 31 December 1991.

investigation into the legality of the independence of the three Baltic countries. The Russian trial on the legal status of their independence is based on the idea that the interim Soviet government in place in 1991 was illegitimate and its decisions therefore also illegitimate.

Since then, the three countries, whose national cultures are clearly northern European rather than Slavic, have been outstanding success stories, implementing economic reforms, and gaining membership of NATO, the European Union (EU), and the United Nations. The Baltic states are located in the northeastern region of Europe, on the eastern shores of the Baltic Sea, bounded on the west and north by the Baltic Sea, which gives the region its name, on the east by Russia, on the southeast by Belarus, and on the southwest by Poland and an exclave of Russia. Figure 3.2 depicts a map of the location of the Baltic States.

Figure 3.2 Location of the Baltic states in Europe

Source: UN (1995).

Transition Countries

Both the CEE and the CIS country blocs are considered transition countries in Europe. These transition economies are economies, which are undergoing a change from a centrally planned economy to a market economy.[6] These economies are undertaking a set of structural transformations intended to develop market-based institutions. These include economic liberalization, where prices are set by market forces rather than by a central planning organization.

In addition, a major effort is placed to remove trade barriers, while pushing to privatize state-owned enterprises and resources. State and collectively run enterprises are restructured as businesses, and a financial sector is created to facilitate macroeconomic stabilization and the movement of private capital.[7] This process is not only being applied in Eastern Bloc countries of Europe, but has also been applied in China, the former Soviet Union and some other emerging and frontier market countries.

The transition process is usually characterized by the change and creation of institutions, particularly private enterprises; changes in the role of the state, thereby, the creation of fundamentally different governmental institutions and the promotion of private-owned enterprises, markets, and independent financial institutions.[8] In essence, one transition mode is the functional restructuring of state institutions from being a provider of growth to an enabler, with the private sector its engine. Due to the different initial conditions during the emerging process of the transition from planned economics to market economics, countries uses different transition model. Countries like China and Vietnam adopted a gradual transition mode, however Russia and some other east-European countries, such as the former Socialist Republic of Yugoslavia, used a more aggressive and quicker paced model of transition. These transition countries in Europe are thus classified today into two political-economic entities: CEE and CIS.

---

[6] Feige (1994).

[7] Feige (1991).

[8] Aristovnik (2006).

The CEE Bloc

As mentioned earlier, the CEE is a bloc of countries comprising Albania, Bulgaria, Croatia, the Czech Republic, Hungary, Poland, Romania, the Slovak Republic, Slovenia, and the three Baltic states: Estonia, Latvia, and Lithuania. But the CEE countries are further subdivided by their accession status to the EU.

The eight first-wave accession countries that joined the EU in May 2004 includes Estonia, Latvia, Lithuania, Czech Republic, Slovakia, Poland, Hungary, and Slovenia. The two second-wave accession countries that joined in January 2007 include Romania and Bulgaria. The third-wave accession country that joined the EU in July 2013 includes Croatia. According to the World Bank,[9] "the transition is over" for the 10 countries that joined the EU in 2004 and 2007, which can be also understood as all countries of the Eastern Bloc.[10]

After 15 years of economic boom in central eastern Europe, during which the countries in the region enjoyed growth levels twice as high as in western Europe, the development came to an abrupt halt as the effects of the global financial crisis that started in 2007. Several states in CEE were struck hard as many of these countries were in a state of rapid development fuelled by foreign direct investment (FDI) inflows when the crisis hit.

More recently, the CEE countries have been showing signs of recovery, some faster than others, reading themselves once again for the numerous opportunities for future economical development. One of the main drivers for economic growth is the regions' great location, opened to a market of over 200 million consumers. In addition, the region enjoys a large qualitative labor force at relatively low costs, which provides an inviting atmosphere for foreign investments and business development. There are still plenty of unexploited opportunities in CEE, whether in its huge surfaces of arable land, in its strong skills in technical and technological areas, numerous investment incentives or unique touristic destinations. Figure 3.3 shows a map of the CEE country blocs.

---

[9] Alam et al. (2008, 42).

[10] OECD (2015).

Figure 3.3 The Central and Eastern Europe country bloc

Source: Stepmap.de

As a whole, the CEE includes the following former socialist countries, which extend east from the border of Germany and south from the
Baltic Sea to the border with Greece: Estonia, Latvia, Lithuania, Czech
Republic, Slovakia, Hungary, Poland, Romania, Bulgaria, Slovenia, Croatia, Albania, Bosnia-Herzegovina, Kosovo, Macedonia, Montenegro, and
Serbia. The fundamental conditions for growth in this region are strong,
especially so in the reform-oriented countries that had introduced business-friendly politics and low tax rates in the run up of their EU accession. In effect, several countries, such as the two largest economies Poland
and Czech Republic but also Slovakia, handled the global financial crisis
surprisingly well. Even the countries hit hardest like Hungary will most

likely turn the crisis into an upswing in a few years time. The growth potential of these countries is also intensified by the integration of CEE countries into the Eurozone and Schengen area.[11] Please refer to Appendix A for a brief scanning of the CEE countries.

Economies at War

This currency crisis challenges in the CEE region (more on this in the next section) are in fact a result of a much bigger threat to the global economy, often dubbed by economists at large as a result of currency wars. For the past few years, at least since 2010, government officials from the G7 economies have been very concerned with the potential escalation of a global economic war. Not a conventional war, with fighter jets, bullets, and bombs, but instead, a "currency war." Finance ministers and central bankers from advanced economies worry that their peers in the G20, which also include several emerging economies, may devalue their currencies to boost exports and grow their economies at their neighbors' expense.

Brazil led the charge, being the first emerging economy to accuse the United States of instigating a currency war in 2010, when the U.S. Federal Reserve bought piles of bonds with newly created money. From a Chinese perspective, with the world's largest holdings of U.S. dollar reserves, a U.S.-lead currency war based on dollar debasement is an American act of default to its foreign creditors, no matter how you disguise it. So far the Chinese have been more diplomatic, but their patience is wearing thin.

These two countries are not alone, as depicted in Figure 3.4, several other emerging markets, such as Saudi Arabia, Korea, Russia, Turkey, and Taiwan, have also been impacted by a weak dollar. That "quantitative easing" (QE) made investors flood emerging markets with hot money in search of better returns, which consequently lifted their exchange rates. But Brazil was not alone, as Japan's Shinzo Abe, the new prime minister,

---

[11] Thomann (2006).

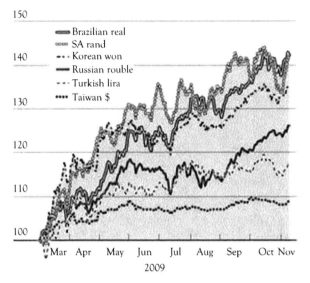

Figure 3.4 Emerging market currencies inflated by weak dollar

Source: Thompson Reuters Datastream.

has also reacted to the QEs in the United States and pledged bold stimulus to restart growth and vanquish deflation in the country.

As advanced economies, like the first three largest world economies—United States, China, and Japan, respectively—try to kick-start their sluggish economies with ultralow interest rates and sprees of money printing, they are putting downward pressure on their currencies. The loose monetary policies are primarily aimed at stimulating domestic demand. But their effects spill over into the currency world.

Japan is facing charges that it is trying first and foremost to lower the value of its currency, the yen, to stimulate its economy and get the edge over other countries. The new government is trying to get Japan, which has been in recession, moving again after a two-decade bout of stagnant growth and deflation. Hence, it has embarked on an economic course it hopes will finally jump-start the economy. The government pushed the Bank of Japan to accept a higher inflation target, which has triggered speculation that the bank will create more money. The prospect of more yen in circulation has been the main reason behind the yen's recent falls to a 21-month low against the dollar and a near 3-year record against the euro.

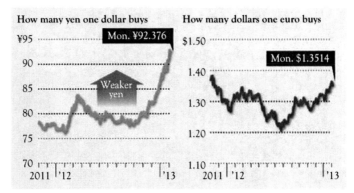

Figure 3.5 Central banks in the United States and Japan has flooded their economies with liquidity

Source: WSJ Market Data Group.

Since Shinzo Abe called for a weaker yen to bolster exports, the currency has fallen by 16 percent against the dollar and 19 percent against the euro. As the yen falls, its exports become cheaper, and those of Asian neighbors South Korea and Taiwan, as well as those countries further afield in Europe, become relatively more expensive. As depicted in Figure 3.5, central banks in the United States and Japan have flooded their economies with liquidity since mid-2012 into 2013, causing the yen and the dollar to weaken against other major currencies.

In our opinion, common sense could prevail, putting an end to the dangerous game of beggar (and blame) thy neighbor. After all, the International Monetary Fund (IMF) was created to prevent such races to the bottom, and should try to broker a truce among foreign exchange competitors. The critical issues in the United States, as well as China and Japan, stem from minimally a blatantly ineffective public policy, but overridingly a failed and destructive economic policy. These policy errors are directly responsible for the opening salvos of the currency war clouds now looming overhead.[12]

---

[12] Our opinion expressed here is from the point of you of international trade and currency exchange as far as it affects international trade, and not from the geopolitical and economic aspects of the issue. We approach the issue of currency wars not from the theoretical, or even simulation models undertaken from behind a desk in an office, but from the point of view of practitioners engaged in international business and foreign trade, on the ground, in four different countries.

So far, Europe has felt the impact of the falling yen the most. At the height of the Eurozone's financial crisis in 2012, the euro was worth $1.21, which was potentially benefitting big exporters like BMW, AUDI, Mercedes, or Airbus. However, at the time of these writing, December 2013, the euro is at $1.38 even though the Eurozone is still the laggard of the world economy.

Across the 17-strong euro area a recovery has got under way following a double-dip recession lasting 18 months, but it is a feeble one. For 2013 as a whole GDP will still continue to fall by 0.4 percent (after declining by 0.6 percent in 2012), but it is expected to rise by 1.1 percent in 2014.[13] A rise in the value of euro, which is also partly to do with the diminishing threat of a collapse of the currency, will do little to help companies in the Eurozone—and will hardly help getting it growing again.

Chinese policymakers reject the conventional thinking proposed by advanced economies. How about the yen's extraordinary rise over the last 40 years, from JPY360 against the dollar at the beginning of the 1970s to about JPY102 today?[14] Not to mention that despite this huge appreciation, Japan's current-account surplus has only got bigger, not smaller. They could also argue that the United States' prescription for China's economic rebalancing, a stronger currency, and a boost to domestic demand, was precisely the policy followed by the Japanese in the late-1980s, leading to the biggest financial bubble in living memory and the 20-year hangover that followed.

Furthermore, the demand by the United States, which is backed by the G7 for a renminbi revaluation, is, in our view, a policy of the United States' default. During the Asian crisis in 1997 to 1998, advanced economies, under the auspices of the IMF, insisted that Asian nations, having borrowed so much, should now tighten their belts. Shouldn't advance economies be doing the same? In addition, Chinese manufacturing margins are so slim that significant change in exchange rates could wipe them out and force layoffs of millions of Chinese. As it is, labor rates are already climbing in China, further squeezing margins. Lastly, a revaluation of the yuan would only push manufacturing to other cheaper emerging markets,

---

[13] The Economist's Writers (2013).

[14] As of December 2013.

such as Vietnam, Cambodia, Thailand, Bangladesh, and other lower pay-ing nations without improving the advanced economies trade deficits.

Notwithstanding, some G7 policymakers believe these grumbles are overdone; arguing that the rest of the world should praise the United States and Japan for such monetary policies, suggesting the Eurozone should do the same. The war rhetoric implies that the United States and Japan are directly suppressing their currencies to boost exports and sup-press imports, which in our view is a zero-sum game, which could degen-erate into protectionism and a collapse in trade.

These countries, however, do not believe such currency devaluation strategy will threaten trade. Instead, their believe seems to be that as cen-tral banks continue to lower their short-term interest rate to near zero, exhausting their conventional monetary methods, they must employ unconventional methods, such as QE, or trying to convince consumers that inflation will raise. Their goal with these actions is to lower real (infla-tion-adjusted) interest rates. If so, inflation should be rising in Japan and in the United States, which according to Figure 3.6 it is.

As Figure 3.6 also shows, over the past decade, Japan has seen the consumer price index (CPI) for most periods hover just below the zero-percent inflation line. The notable exceptions were in 2008, when infla-tion rose as high as 2 percent, and in late 2009, when prices fell at close

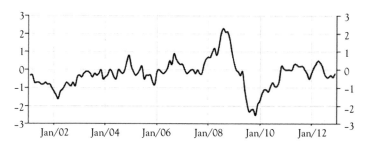

Figure 3.6 Japan's inflation rate has been climbing since 2010 as a result of economic stimulus

Source: Trading Economics,[15] Japan's Ministry of Internal Affairs and Communications.

---

[15] www.tradingeconomics.com (accessed December 9, 2013).

to a 2 percent rate. The rise in inflation coincided with a crash in capital spending. The worst period of deflation preceded an upturn. Of course, the preceding figure does not provide enough data to infer causal effects, but it seem, however, that the relationship between growth and Japan's mild deflation may be more complicated than the Great Depression-inspired deflationary spiral narrative suggests. The principal goal of this policy was to stimulate domestic spending and investment, but lower real rates usually weaken the currency as well, and that in turn tends to depress imports. Nevertheless if the policy is successful in reviving domestic demand, it will eventually lead to higher imports.

At least that's how the argument goes. The IMF actually concluded that the United States' first rounds of QE boosted its trading partners' output by as much as 0.3 percent. The dollar did weaken, but that became a motivation for Japan's stepped-up assault on deflation. The combined monetary boost on opposite sides of the Pacific has been a powerful elixir for global investor confidence, if anything, to move hot money onto emerging markets where the interests were much higher than at advanced economies.

The reality is that most advanced economies have over-consumed in recent years. It has too many debts. But rather than dealing with those debts—living a life of austerity, accepting a period of relative stagnation—these economies want to shift the burden of adjustment on to its creditors, even when those creditors are relatively poor nations with low per capita incomes. This is true not only for Chinese but also for many other countries in Asia and in other parts of the emerging world. During the Asian crisis in 1997 to 1998, Western nations, under the auspices of the IMF, insisted that Asian nations, having borrowed too much, should now tighten their belts. But the United States doesn't seem to think it should abide by the same rules. Far better to use the exchange rate to pass the burden on to someone else than to swallow the bitter pill of austerity.

Meanwhile, European policymakers, fearful that their countries' exports are caught in this currency war crossfire, have entertained unwise ideas such as directly managing the value of the euro. While the option of generating money out of thin air may not be available to emerging markets, where inflation tends to remain a problem, limited capital controls may be a sensible short-term defense against destabilizing inflows

Figure 3.7 In 2009 emerging markets significantly outperformed advanced (developed) economies

Source: FTSE All-World Indices.

of hot money. Figure 3.7 illustrates how the inflows of hot-money leaving advanced economies in search of better returns on investments in emerging markets have caused these markets to significantly outperform advanced (developed) markets.

Currency War May Cause Damage to Global Economy

As more countries try to weaken their currencies for economic gain, there may come a point where the fragile global economic recovery could be derailed and the international financial system thrown into chaos. That's why financial representatives from the world's leading 20 industrial and developing nations, spent most of their time during the G20 summit in Moscow in September 2013.

In our view, policymakers are focusing on the wrong issue. Rather than focus on currency manipulation, all sides would be better served to zero in on structural reforms. The effects of that would be far more beneficial in the long run than unilateral United States, China, or Japan currency action, and more sustainable. The G20 should focus on a comprehensive package centered on structural reforms in all countries, both advanced economies and emerging markets. Exchange rates should be an important part of that package, no doubt. For instance, to reduce the current-account deficits of the United States, Americans must save more. To continue to simply devalue the dollar will not be sufficient for that purpose. Likewise, China's current-account surpluses were caused by a broad set of domestic economic distortions, from state-allocated credit to artificially low interest rates. Correcting China's external imbalances requires eliminating all of these distortions as well.

As long as policymakers continue to focus on currency exchange issues, the volatility in the currency markets will continue to escalate. It actually has become so worrisome that the G7 advanced economies have warned that volatile movements in exchange rates could adversely hit the global economy. Figure 3.8 provides a broad view (rebased at 100 percent on August 1, 2008) of main exchange rates against the dollar.

When it became clear that Shinzo Abe and his agenda of growth-at-all-costs would win Japan's elections, the yen lost more than 10 percent

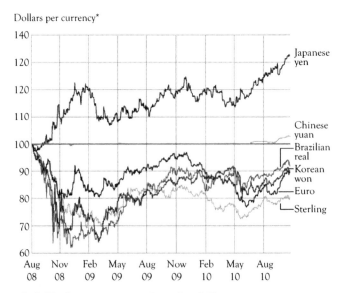

Figure 3.8 Exchange rates against the dollar

Source: Bloomberg.

against the dollar and some 15 percent against the euro. In turn, the dollar has also plumbed to its lowest level against the euro in nearly 15 months. These monetary debasement strategies are adversely impacting and angering export-driven countries such as Brazil, and many of the Brazil, Russia, India, China, and South Africa (BRICS), Association of Southeast Nations (ASEAN), Colombia, Indonesia, Vietnam, Egypt, Turkey, and South Africa (CIVETS) and Middle East—North Africa (MENA) blocs. But they also are stirring the pot in Europe. The Eurozone has largely sat out this round of monetary stimulus and now finds itself in the invidious position of having a contracting economy and a rising currency.

James Rickards, author of *Currency Wars: The Making of the Next Global Crisis*, expect the international monetary system to destabilize and collapse. In his views, "there will be so much money-printing by so many central banks that people's confidence in paper money will wane, and inflation will rise sharply."[16]

If policymakers truly want to stage off this currency war, then it is a matter of doing what it was done in 1985 with the Plaza Accord.[17] This time, however, we will need a different version, as it will not be about the United States and the G5 of the time, in 1985. It will have to be an *Asian Plaza Accord* under the support and auspices of the G20. It will have to be about the Asia export led and mercantilist leadership agreeing amongst them. The chances of this happening, of advanced economies seeing the requirement for it, or these economies relinquishing its powers in any measurable fashion are not at all possible under the current political gamesmanship presently being played.

---

[16] Guerrera (2013).

[17] The Plaza Accord was an agreement between the governments of France, West Germany, Japan, the United States, and the United Kingdom, to depreciate the U.S. dollar in relation to the Japanese yen and German Deutsche Mark by intervening in currency markets. The five governments signed the accord on September 22, 1985 at the Plaza Hotel in New York City.

CHAPTER 4

The Economic Impact of Integration of CEE Economies

Overview

The integration of Central and Eastern Europe (CEE) countries with the West, in particularly the European Union (EU) is expected to produce significant benefits to all of these economies in transition. Along with the effects on gross domestic product (GDP originated from changes in tariffs, accession to the EU internal market and free labor movement), consumption and terms of trade, as well as the absorption of EU funds could help the process of convergence and catching up.

This chapter is a discussion, from our point of view, of the economic impact and challenges being promoted by the EU enlargement into CEE economies, and how it has contributed to these countries economic growth. We took in consideration macroeconomic variables such as rate of economic growth, the progress of market or structural reforms, economic freedom, foreign aid, and the foreign direct investment (FDI) inflow.

Economic integration may also be interpreted and measured in by comparing GDP per capita in current international dollars, in purchasing power parity (PPP) terms of each CEE country with that of an advanced economy in the EU, such as Germany, due to its role as the largest EU national economy and major economic and trade partner of most of CEE economies on the one hand, and its largely positive but rather modest rate of growth in 2000s and 2010s.[1]

---

[1] For the most part our analyses were based on based on the IMF World Economic Outlook October 2014 database statistics. But a few other sources we used and cited throughout this chapter.

Of course, there are many other variables that need to be taken into consideration, such as leveraging diversity—natural, cultural, political, ethnic, and religious—among these countries, that were for the most part omitted, as not to detract from the macroeconomic focus of this book. We did consider, however, the possible impacts of EU structural funds on FDI inflows into the region, under the circumstances of how diverse each country in CEE is, not only on the stage of transition of their economies but also on the different absorption rates for both exports and imports, as well as the potential adverse effects that the current global financial crisis could have in this process, which may affect the prospects for all economies of that region.

Economic Growth

Since the collapse of communism in the former Soviet Union, a number of CEE countries have been faced with the prospect of transforming their economy from a central-planned to a market-oriented one. Various researches and reviewed literature[2] (see partial list at the footnote) seem to agree that, overall, the integration of the CEE economies into the EU has significantly contributed to economic growth of those countries that have already joined the EU.

As discussed in earlier chapters, the transformation of these economies has been aided by the privatization of state-owned enterprises (SOEs) and the development of the private business sector, in which FDI inflows have been playing a major role not only in the privatization of SOEs but also in the restructuring process of these economies.[3] The end of communism and the advanced economic integration of Europe have forever shaped global development in the twenty-first century.

The CEE countries recognize the importance of FDI in the development and modernization of their economies. The FDI inflows into the CEE economies have in fact been a vital force in the first stage of the privatization process during the transition period. It has increased in

---

[2] Kapacki and Prochiniak (2009); Zaman (2008); Dabrowski (2015); Mühlberger and Körner (2014); Rozmahel et al. (2013).
[3] Case and Fair (2004).

the past 20 years to become the most common type of capital flow needed for stabilization and economic growth,[4] with the CEE countries actively seeking to attract and promote FDI inflows to liberalize their economies and safeguard free movement of capital and profits.

As most of the privatization and restructuring process comes to an end, however, FDI inflows remains an important factor, but for a different purpose. Attracting FDI has become a major national strategy for these countries as FDI is seen as an essential factor in, among others, stimulating economic growth and expanding capital. Hence, a higher inflow of FDI in the region is becoming ever more important for the advancement of the globalization processes in CEE, including the boosting of productivity, stimulating the job market and employment, fostering innovation and technology transfer, and the enhancement of sustained economic growth.

In the economic arena, it integrates national economies with the global economy. The global economy itself is in a state of transition, ranging from a set of strong national economies to a set of interlinking trade groups. This transition has accelerated over the past few years with the collapse of communism and the coalescing of the European trading nations into a single market. One of the most important paths driving global development into the twenty-first century is the advanced economic integration of Europe. It has been an essential factor contributing to the growth of FDI in the CEE countries over the past few years. Never before have so many economies been open to global trade and finance flow then now, after the liberalization of the former communist economies.[5]

Looking at the period between 2001 and 2013, from the end of the dramatic period of transition-related restructuring and related prolonged output decline through mid-1990s, as well as the series of emerging-market crises in the second half of 1990s, which affected part of the region, the impact of integration is very visible, although not always positive. Based on Dabrowski's analysis,[6] Figure 4.1 provides a glimpse of such impact of integration in the current EU members, including Croatia, which joined the EU in July 2013.

---

[4] Kornecki (2010).
[5] De la Dehesa (2006).
[6] Dabrowski (2014).

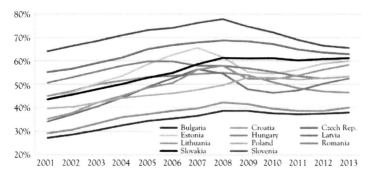

Figure 4.1 GDP per capita in current international $, PPP adjusted, Germany = 100%, 2001–2013, for EU new member states

Source: Dabrowski (2014).

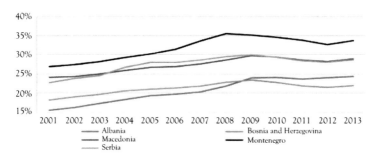

Figure 4.2 GDP per capita in current international $, PPP adjusted, Germany = 100%, 2001–2013, for Western Balkan countries

Source: Dabrowski (2014).

Also according to Dabrowski's analysis,[7] Figure 4.2 provides an overview of GDP growth for the EU actual and potential country candidates in the Western Balkan region, except Kosovo for which the respective data was not available.

In both country groups depicted in Figures 4.1 and 4.2, one can clearly distinguish two subperiods, one until 2007 and 2008 with rapid catching up as a result of the convergence from a central-planned to a market-driven economy, and another after 2008 with either deconvergence or no progress in further convergence.

_____

[7] Dabrowski (2014).

Some of the main factors behind this rapid convergence experienced through 2007 and 2008 include the post-transition growth recovery, the joining of the single European market, or partial access to it, in the case of EU candidates, and the global economic boom, which resulted in large-scale FDI inflows throughout the region. Also noticeable from Figures 4.1 and 4.2 is the fact that when the global financial crisis stroke the region from 2008 to 2009, and even earlier in the Baltic countries (2007), the convergence trajectory turned negative pretty much everywhere.[8]

However, we can distinguish substantial differences across both country subgroups. The four new EU-member states with the highest income per-capita level in early 2000s, including Slovenia, Czech Republic, Hungary, and Croatia, had recorded a continuous decline in their relative GDP per capita levels, as compared to Germany after 2008. The three Baltic countries experienced an even sharper decline from 2008 to 2010 but then returned to rapid reconvergence, even though only Lithuania has managed to exceed its precrisis convergence level so far. The somewhat similar growth pattern, where there is a decline in GDP then a recovery, can be observed in most Western Balkan EU-candidate countries, except for Albania. The same was true for Romania and Bulgaria although with smaller scales of changes in their convergence trajectories, particularly for Bulgaria. Lastly, Poland, Slovakia, and Albania managed to continue their convergence vis-à-vis Germany after 2008 although at a very slow pace.

Growth Challenges

Looking ahead, one must ask what kind of challenges will be faced by CEE countries in their future development, and whether they will have chance to return to their pre-2007 and 2008 convergence trajectory. Clearly the preglobal financial crisis growth bonanza based on large-scale capital inflow is unlikely to return anytime soon. We now live in a much different world. Risks and challenges threatening the CEE countries continue growth and path to prosperity are many. The following are only a few main ones we find important.

---

[8] In Hungary, conversion stopped in 2005.

The demographic trends of the region will continue to be progressively unfavorable, as a result of the declining cohorts of working-age populations. Although this is a common European problem even for Germany, the eastern part of the region may very well experience sharper decline in this respect than their higher-income Western European neighbors.

However, the region will likely face even more dramatic challenges with respect to capital inflows and investments as a whole. The short-term investment boom of 2003 to 2007 was largely based on imported savings, which caused large current account imbalances. Unfortunately, the gross saving rate in the CEE countries is very low, in the range of 16 to 17 percent of GDP, the lowest among emerging-market regions and much lower as compared with the Eurozone,[9] as depicted in Figure 4.3, which has not improved after the global financial crisis as one would have expected. Without an increase in the gross saving rate, the CEE countries will continue to have to rely on ever larger-scale import of saving, in the range of 8 to 10 percent of GDP annually. Such massive net capital inflow seems very unlikely in the postcrisis environment of financial deleveraging. The size of net FDI has been much smaller and declining in recent years. Needless to say, excessive reliance on short-term capital inflows may increase external macroeconomic vulnerability in the case of adverse shocks, as several countries learned in 2008 to 2009. When

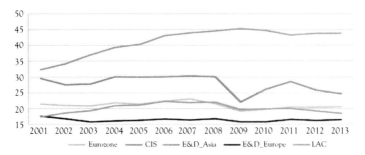

Figure 4.3 Gross national savings, % of GDP, interregional comparison, 2001–2013

Source: Dabrowski (2014).

---

[9] Dabrowski (2014).

capital inflows came to a halt in 2008 the investment rate also turned downward, especially in the Baltics, Bulgaria, and part of the Western Balkans.

Overall there has been significant recovery since 2009, but it may not be sustainable due to other challenges that may lay ahead, including among many of the geopolitical and macroeconomic factors, the indebtedness of the advanced economies, currency wars, control of capital flows and currency rate, and the control of inflation. These challenges are discussed next.

Indebtedness of the Advanced Economies

Canadian Prime Minister, Stephen Harper, in September of 2013, was vehemently urging G-20 leaders not to lose sight of the vital importance of reining in debt across the group after several years of deficit-fuelled stimulus spending, sticking to a common refrain in the face of weak recoveries among member countries including Canada. Harper's concern regarding the risks of accumulating public debt was not without merits. Harper also acknowledged that recoveries from the financial crisis have been disappointing because many of the advanced economies continue to grapple with high unemployment, weak growth, and rising income inequality.

In the United States, since the economic crisis of 2008, financial analysts and politicians have been very vocal with ideas of *fiscal cliffs*, debt ceiling, and defaults. To some extent, the situation is not much different among the EU region, and contagion is spreading through the CEE. Debt-to-GDP ratios and deficit figures have been touted as omens of financial failure and public debt has been heralded as the harbinger of apocalypse. The truth of the matter is that many countries around the world, especially in the emerging markets during the 1970s and 1980s, have experienced large amounts of debt, in excess of 100 percent of GDP, as advanced economies are experiencing right now. Nonetheless, what is different this time, is that while the CEE, had most of their debt in external markets, denominated in foreign currencies, they also, as transition economies, have differing structures and institutions than the advanced economies.

When we look at the last quarter of the nineteenth century, it was a period of large accumulation of debt due to widespread infrastructure building in advanced economies around the globe, mainly due to the new innovation at the time, such as the railroads. As these economies expanded and continued to invest in infrastructure, much debt was also created. The same was true during the World War I (WWI), reflecting the military spending taken on during the wartime period, and immediately after that during the reconstruction period. Then came another period of large creation of debt, during the and after the World War II (WWII). In this case, some of these debt levels started to build a bit earlier, as a result of the great recession, but most were the result of WWII. Lastly, we have the period where most governments and policymakers of advanced economies struggled to move from the old economic systems to the current one. During these four different periods, most advanced economies experienced 100 percent or more debt-to-GDP ratios at least one or more of times. The dynamics of debt-to-GDP ratios are in fact very diverse; their effects are widely varied, and based on a variety of factors. Take for example the case of the United Kingdom in 1918, the United States in 1946, Belgium in 1983, Italy in 1992, Canada in 1995, and Japan in 1997. All of these countries went through a process of indebtedness, each with a full range of outcomes.

In the case of England, policymakers tried to return to the gold standard at pre-WWI levels to restore trade, prosperity and prestige, and to also pay off as much debt, as quickly as possible to preserve the image of British good credit. They sought to achieve these goals through policies that included austerity. Their efforts did not have the intended effects. The dual pursuit of going back to a strengthened currency from a devalued one and the pursuit of fiscal austerity seemed to be a deciding factor in the failure. Trying to go back to the gold standard that had not depreciated made British exports less attractive than those of surrounding countries who had not chosen this path. Consequently, exports were low, and to combat this, British banks kept interest rates high. Those high interest rates meant that the debt the country was trying to pay off increased in value and the country's slow growth and austerity did not give them the economic power to pay the debts off as they wanted to. In trying to maintain integrity and the image of "Old Faithful Britain," the policymakers ruined their chances for swift recovery.

In the United States, policymakers chose to not control inflation, and kept a floor on government bonds. Over time, these ideas changed and bond protection measures were lifted while the government's ability to intervene in inflation situations was changed. The United States experienced rapid growth during this time, partially due to high levels of monetary inflation, but that inflation, even though it would "burst" at the start of the Korean War, allowed the United States to pay off much of its debt. This, coupled with the floor on U.S. bonds, created a favorable post high debt level scenario.

Japan's initial response to its situation was the cutting of inflation rates and the introduction of fiscal stimulus programs. This did not have the intended effect, as currency appreciated. The underlying issues that had helped to cause the high debt-to-GDP ratios were still present, and would be until 2001, when the government committed to changing policy and structure in focused ways in order to boost the country's economy. Japan still has a very high debt-to-GDP ratio, but the weaknesses in the banking sector have been fixed, and the country seems to be on a path to recovery.

Italy's attempts at fiscal reform included changes to many social programs, including large cuts to pension spending. The reforms, though, were not implemented quickly enough and did not address enough of the demographic issues to make a large impact. It wasn't until later that further fiscal consolidation was achieved. Important to note with Italy is that GDP growth did not help to reduce debt at this period, as it remained very weak.

Belgium used similar kinds of fiscal consolidation plans to those of Italy, but those plans were more widespread and implemented at a more rapid pace. The relative success of these initial fiscal consolidations helped to further growth and reduction of the Belgian debt ratio, fueling another round of successful consolidation when the country needed it to enter the EU.

Canada's initial reaction included fiscal changes such as tax hikes and spending cuts, a plan of austerity. The plan failed and deepened the country's debt. The second wave of fiscal consolidation was aimed at fixing some of the structural imbalances that had caused the debt levels in the first place. It worked, helped along by the strengthening of economic conditions in surrounding countries, mainly the United States. The Canada example shows that the external conditions are just as important in success as the policies or missions taken on within the country experiencing high debt ratios.

From all of these examples, we can have an idea of the impact that advanced economies have on each other and on the CEE economies as well. In an intertwined global economy, imbalances in one country's economy impacts virtually every other country in the world, although the impact and mitigation of such impacts will always vary depending on internal and external market conditions, as well as policy development. Similar solutions, like the allowing of inflation in the United States, may not work today, or in another country. For instance, if we take the global financial crises that started in 2008, allowing inflation to rise to higher levels could pose risks to the financial institutions, and could lead to a less globally integrated financial system.

The most pertinent choice of example would appear to be the kinds of fiscal policy used in Canada, Belgium, and Italy. All three countries attempted to achieve low inflation, but the other policy reforms of the countries varied in success. More permanent fiscal changes tend to create more prominent and lasting reductions to debt levels, and even then the country must be exposed to increased external demand for the recovery of that country to be similar to the successful cases cited earlier. Consolidation needs to be implemented alongside measures to support growth and changes that address structural issues. The final factor to note is that even with a successful plan, the effects of that plan take time. No reduction in debt levels will be quick in today's global and interweaved economies.

The Crisis Isn't Over Yet

Advanced economies, specifically in the EU and the United States, are still dealing with the global financial crises that started sometime in 2008. Despite the positive rhetoric of policymakers and government on both sides of the Atlantic, according to the Harvard Economist Carmen Reinhart, the crisis is not yet over. She alleges that both the U.S. Federal Reserve and the European Central Bank (ECB) are keeping interest rates low to help governments out of their debt crises. As in the past, and the aforecited examples in history, central banks are bending over backwards to help governments of advanced economies to finance their deficits.

Nowadays, however, monetary policy is doing the job, but unlike many policymakers would like us to believe, these economies seldom are able to just grow themselves out of debt. Money to pay for these debts must come from somewhere. Reinhart[10] believes those advanced economies in debt today must adopt a combination of austerity to restrain the trend of adding to the stack of debt and higher inflation, which is effectively a subtle form of taxation, which consequently will cause a depreciation of the currency, eroding people's savings.

We do not advocate against or in favor of current central bank policies in these economies, which is not the scope of this book on the first place. Advanced economies, however, need to deal with their debt one way or another, as these high debt levels prevents growth and freezes the financial system and the credit process. This too impacts CEE economies in a very negative way, at least as long as these markets continue to heavily depend on the exports to these advanced economies and FDI inflows. We do believe, however, that the indebtedness of the United States and the EU, in particular, affects the CEE economies in a major way, and that current central bank policies are not effective, as money is being transferred from responsible savers to borrowers via negative interest rates.

In other words, when the inflation rate is higher than the interest rates paid in the markets, the debts shrink as if by magic. As dubbed by Ronald McKinnon,[11] the term *financial repression* describes various policies that allow governments to *capture* and *underpay* domestic savers. Such policies include forced lending to governments by pension funds and other domestic financial institutions, interest-rate caps, capital controls, and many more. Typically, governments use a mixture of these policies to bring down debt levels, but inflation and financial repression usually only work for domestically held debt—although the Eurozone is a special hybrid case. This financial repression being used by advanced economies, designed to avoid an explicit default on the debt, is not only ineffective in the long run but also not fair to responsible taxpayers, and eventually may entice public revolts such as the ones already witnessed in Greece and Spain. Governments could write off part of the debt, but evidently

---

[10] Dabrowski (2014).
[11] McKinnon (1973).

no politician will be willing to spearhead such write-offs. After all, most citizens do not realize their savings are being eroded and that there is a major transfer of wealth taking place. Undeniably, advanced economies around the world have a problem with debt. In the past, several tactics, including financial repression, have dealt with such problems, and now it seems, it is resurging again in the wake of the global and Eurozone crises.

Financial repression, coupled with a steady dose of inflation, cuts debt burdens from two directions. First is by introducing low nominal interest rates, which reduce debt-servicing costs. Then trough negative real interest rates, which erodes the debt-to-GDP ratio; in other words, this is a tax on savers. Financial repression also has some noteworthy political-economic properties. Unlike other taxes, the "repression" tax rate is determined by financial regulations and inflation performance that are obscure to the highly politicized realm of fiscal measures. Given that deficit reduction usually involves highly unpopular expenditure reductions and tax increases of one form or another, the relatively *stealthier* financial repression tax may be a more politically palatable alternative for authorities faced with the need to reduce outstanding debts. In such environment, inflation, by historic standards, does not need to take market participants entirely by surprise, as it doesn't need to be very high.

Unlike the United States, which is resorting to financial repression, Europe is focusing more on austerity measures; despite the fact inflation is still at a low level. Notwithstanding, debt restructuring, inflation, and financial repression, are not a substitute for austerity. All these measures reduce a country's existing stock of debt, and as argued by Reinhart,[12] policymakers need a combination of both to bring down debt to a sustainable level. Although the United States is very highly indebted, an advantage it has against all other advanced economies is that foreign central banks are then ones holding most of its debts.

It is obvious the currently very uncertain situation in the Eurozone, for which the leading indicators are pointing to a period of recession, while the sovereign debt crisis continues to escalate from one episode to the next, also has negative ramifications for CEE. In fact, back in 2012,

---

[12] Reinhart and Kirkegaard (2012).

the Austrian Raiffeisen Bank International AG[13] significantly lowered its 2012 growth forecasts for most of the countries in the CEE region, resulting in a GDP growth estimate of 2.3 percent for the region as a whole, anticipating a slowdown of GDP growth for the region. The good news is that, as mentioned earlier, even though growth in CEE is slowing down, the rate remains significantly higher than that expected for the Eurozone and advanced economies as a whole. It is also expected that the CEE region will continue its catch-up process toward the Eurozone with a positive growth through 2015.

We believe that the combination of high public and private debts in the advanced economies and the perceived dangers of currency misalignments and overvaluation in CEE countries facing surges in capital inflows, which in turn are causing pressures toward currency intervention and capital controls, interact to produce a home-bias in finance and a resurgence of financial repression. At present, we find that CEE economies are being forced to adopt similar policies as the advanced economies—hence the *currency wars*—but not as a financial repression, but more in the context of *macroprudential* regulations.

Advanced economies are developing financial regulatory measures to keep international capital out of CEE, and emerging markets as a whole, and in advanced economies. Such economic controls are intended to counter loose monetary policy in the advanced economies and discourage the so-called *hot money*,[14] while regulatory changes in advanced economies are meant to create a captive audience for domestic debt. This offers advanced and emerging market economies, including CEE economies, common ground on tighter restrictions on international financial flows, which borderlines protectionism policies. More broadly, the world is witnessing a return to more tightly regulated domestic financial environment, in other words, financial repression.

---

[13] www.rbinternational.com/eBusiness/01_template1/829189266947841370-829189148030934104_829602608694921416-829188181663843300-NA-2-EN.html

[14] Capital that is frequently transferred between financial institutions in an attempt to maximize interest or capital gain.

Therefore, we believe advanced economies are imposing a major strain on global financial markets, in particularly on CEE economies by way of exporting inflation to those countries, because governments are incapable of reducing their debts, pressuring central banks to get involved in an attempt to resolve the crisis. Reinhart argues that such policy does not come cheap, and those responsible citizens, those everyday savers, will be the ones feeling the consequences of such policies the most; they will pay the price. While no central bank will admit it is keeping interest rates low to help governments out of their debt crises, they are doing whatever they can to help these economies finance their deficits.

The major danger of such a central bank policy, which can be at first very detrimental to CEE economies who are still largely dependent on consumer exports demands from advanced economies, is that it can lead to high inflation. As inflation rises among advanced economies, it is also exported to CEE economies and other emerging markets. In other words, as the U.S. dollar and the euro debases and loses buying power, CEE markets experience an artificial strengthening of their currency, courtesy of the U.S. Federal Reserve and the ECB, causing the prices of their goods and services to also increase, hurting exports in the process.

No doubt, a critical factor explaining the high incidence of negative real interest rates in the wake of the crisis is the aggressively expansive stance of monetary policy, particularly the official central bank interventions in many advanced and emerging economies during this period. At the time of these writings, winter 2016, the levels of public debt in many advanced economies is at their highest levels, with some of these economies even face the prospect of debt restructuring. Moreover, public and private external debts, which we should not ignore are typically a volatile source of funding, are at historic highs, while the high and persistent levels of unemployment in many advanced economies persist. These negative trends offer further motivation for central banks and policymakers to keep interest rates low, posing renewed taste for financial repression. Hence, we believe the final crisis isn't over yet. The impact such advanced economies are imposing on emerging markets, and its own economies, is only the tip of a very large iceberg.

Currency Wars

Currency war, also known as competitive devaluation of currency, is a term raised as the alarm by Brazil's former Finance Minister Guido Mantega to describe the 2010 effort by the United States and China to have the lowest value of their currencies.[15] The rationale behind a currency war is really quite simple. By devaluing one's currency, it makes exports more competitive, assists individual country to capture a greater share of global trade, and boosts its economy. Greater exports mean employing more workers and therefore helping improve economic growth rates, even at the eventual cost of inflation and unrest.

In currency wars, exchange rate manipulation can be accomplished in several ways:

- Direct Intervention—Adopted by the People's Bank of China (PBOC) and Bank of Japan (BOJ), in which a country can sell its own currency in order to buy foreign currencies, resulting in a direct devaluation of its currency on a relative basis.
- Quantitative Easing (QE)—Taken by U.S. Federal Reserve, in which a country can use its own currency to buy its own sovereign debt, or effectively foreign debt, and ultimately depreciate its currency.
- Interest Rates—Exercised by BOJ, U.S. Federal Reserve and ECB, in which a country can lower its interest rates and thereby create downward pressure on its currency, since it becomes cheaper to borrow against others.
- Threats of Devaluation—Used by the United States toward China, in which a country can threaten to take any of the previous actions along with other measures and occasionally achieve the desired devaluation in the open market.

The United States allows its currency, the dollar, to devalue by expansionary fiscal and monetary policies. It's doing this through increasing

---

[15] Amadeo (2013).

spending, thereby increasing the debt, and by keeping the Fed funds rate at virtually zero, increasing credit and the money supply. More importantly, through QE, it has been printing money to buy bonds, currently at $85 billion a month.

China tries to keep its currency low by pegging it to the dollar, along with a basket of other currencies. It keeps the peg by buying U.S. Treasuries, which limits the supply of dollars, thereby strengthening it. This keeps Chinese yuan low by comparison. Obviously, both the United States and China were able to benefit from currency rate manipulation to secure their leading positions in the international trade.

According to the World Trade Organization (WTO) International Trade Statistics 2013, the United States is still the world's biggest trader in merchandise, with imports and exports totaling $ 3,881 billion in 2012. Its trade deficit amounts to $ 790 billion, 4.9 percent of its GDP. China follows closely behind the United States, with merchandise trade totaling $ 3,867 billion in 2012. China's trade surplus was $ 230 billion, or 2.8 percent of its GDP.

Through manipulation of currency rate, devaluation is also used to cut real debt levels by reducing the purchasing power of a nation's debt held by foreign investors, which works especially well for the United States. But such currency rate manipulation has invited destructive retaliation in the form of tit-for-tat currency war among the world's largest economies. A joint statement issued by the Japanese government and the BOJ in January 2013 stated that the central bank would adopt a 2 percent inflation target. Later on, Haruhiko Kuroda, the BOJ's Governor announced the BOJ's boldest attempt so far to stimulate Japan's economy and end years of deflation. The bank intends to double the amount of money in circulation by buying about ¥13 trillion in financial assets, including some ¥2 trillion in government bonds, every month as long as necessary. BOJ's effort together with the months of anticipation that preceded it has knocked the yen down sharply against the dollar and other major currencies, as shown in Figure 4.4, and sparked a rally in Japanese shares. But it has also further reignited fears of currency tensions around.

The EU made its move in 2013, to boost its export and fight deflation. The ECB, after cutting its policy rate to 0.5 percent in May, lowered

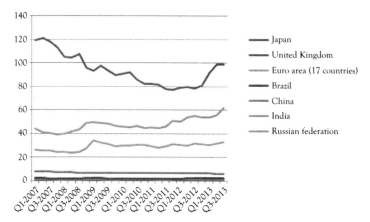

Figure 4.4 Currency exchange rates, national units per $ (quarterly average)

Sources: OECD Main Economic Indicators (MEI) database.

such rate further to 0.25 percent on November 7, 2013. This immediately drove down the euro to dollar conversion rate to $1.3366.

Such strategy should be of concern to CEE countries because the currency wars are driving their currencies higher, by comparison. This raises the prices of commodities, which fuels their manufacturing industry, their primary exports. This makes CEE countries less competitive, and slows their economic growth. In fact, according to Brezinschek, Raiffeisen Research's chief analyst, the impacts on CEE stem both from the region's lopsided export-orientation where up to 85 percent of CEE total exports go to the EU, as well as the tensions within the European banking sector. However, Brezinschek expects the effects in the Commonwealth of Independent States (CIS) region to be less pronounced than in the CEE, due to the more robust domestic demand in the CIS countries. Raiffeisen Research also expects the CIS region's GDP to grow at higher levels than CEE region through 2015.

Control of Capital Flows and Currency Rate

To avoid the repeat of such painful history and damage to international trade caused by ongoing currency war, Pascal Lamy, former

Director-General of WTO, pointed out that "the international community needs to make headway on the issue of reform of the international monetary system. Unilateral attempts to change or retain the status quo will not work," in the opening session of the WTO Seminar on Exchange Rates and Trade on March 27, 2012.

The key challenge to the rest of the world is the U.S. policy of renewed QE, which gives both potential benefits and increasing pressure to other countries. Among the benefits would be to help push back the risk of deflation that has been observed in much of the advanced world. Avoiding stagnation or renewed recession in advanced economies, such as the EU and the United States, in turn, would be a major benefit for CEE countries, whose economic cycles remain closely correlated with those in the developed world.[16] Another major plus would be to greatly reduce the threat of protectionism, particularly in the United States itself. The most plausible scenario for advanced economies protectionism would be precisely a long period of deflation and economic stagnation, as seen in the 1930s.[17]

Based on our observation, the adjustment issue has been relatively easier in other advanced economies, especially countries within the EU, that are also experiencing high unemployment and are threatened by deflation. In this situation, there could be a rationale not so much for a currency war as for a coordinated monetary easing across developed countries to help fend off deflation while also reducing the risk of big exchange rate realignments among the major developed economies.

In contrast, it is more complicated for most CEE economies, as the EU enlargement brings more benefits to new entry member states and only a modest improvement for the old EU member states.[18] On the other hand, we cannot overlook that, into an integrated economic group of countries with different levels of economic and social development such as in the CEE, those more advanced benefit to a greater extent of the integration effects compared with the less developed ones. This latter view takes into consideration the positive effects of repatriated profits

---

[16] Canuto (2010).
[17] Canuto and Giugale (2010).
[18] Lejour and Nahuis (2004).

generated by the large volume of FDI in CEE countries, by the earnings in the developed countries on the account of the foreign labor which is paid less compared with local workers, by the opportunities for increased production in these countries as a result of new markets opening in the new member states, and so on. Some countries, such as Poland and Lithuania, may experience relatively stronger growth and higher inflationary rather than deflationary pressures. In this situation, the U.S. monetary easing poses more challenging policy choices by creating added stimulus for capital inflows to CEE economies, flows that have already been surging since 2010 through 2008, when the global financial crisis ensued, which was caused by both high short-term interest rate spreads and the stronger long-term growth prospects of CEE economies. To put currency rate and capital flow under reasonable control with the increasing pressure from U.S. monetary easing, there are three approaches suggested by the World Bank experts.[19]

First is to maintain a fixed exchange rate peg and an open capital account while giving up control of monetary policy as an independent policy instrument. This approach tends to suit economies such as Latvia, Lithuania, Bulgaria, and Bosnia and Herzegovina, highly integrated both economically and institutionally with the larger economies of the EU to whose exchange rates are pegged. It is less appropriate, however, for larger economies such as Poland, whose domestic cycles may not be at the same pace as of the even much larger economies of the EU or the United States, in which the zloty was pegged.

In Poland's situation, in May 1991, the government sharply devalued the zloty and switched the peg from the U.S. dollar to a five-currency basket. Poland quickly realized that importing loose U.S. monetary policy tended to stimulate excessive domestic money growth, inflation in the goods market, and speculative bubbles in asset markets. By October, the end had come for a fixed exchange rate that everyone had to admit was not working. Starting in that month, the Polish authorities replaced the fixed exchange rate with a crawling peg. Under that system, the exchange rate of the zloty was fixed in relation to the five-currency basket on a

---

[19] Brahmbhatt, Canuto, and Ghosh (2010).

day-to-day basis, but at a rate that steadily depreciated. The rate of depreciation, initially 1.8 percent per month, was kept below the prevailing rate of inflation and gradually slowed as the economy stabilized. After 2000, Poland followed a policy that combined a floating exchange rate with inflation targeting. From 2001 to 2011, inflation was respectably moderate, averaging just fewer than 3 percent per year. The floating exchange rate largely absorbed external shocks and changes in financial flows without undue damage to the real economy.[20]

Second is to pursue independent monetary policies that target the CEE economies' own inflation and activity levels, combined with relatively flexible exchange rates and open capital accounts, as Poland actually did, and which a growing number of CEE economies have been moving toward. Given rising inflation pressures, the appropriate monetary policy in many CEE markets at present would likely be to tighten, which will however attract even more capital inflows and further appreciate exchange rates. In fact, the Organization for Economic Cooperation and Development (OECD)[21] expects the CIS and the CEE economies to advance in 2015 and 2016 after a mixed picture in the past few years as the region tries to overcome the impact of a slump in the Eurozone.

We believe Russia has very little leeway to cut interest rates while Hungary will likely keep interests on hold, even though Poland may start removing its monetary policy stimulus. We also believe Slovenia will continue to work on repairing its bank balance sheets and shoring up the sector, since in our views, this is the most pressing task the country has to undertake in to stabilize its economy. Sustained appreciation raises concerns about loss of export competitiveness and sometimes may lead to contentious structural adjustments in the real economy. So countries may also fear that large appreciations will undercut their long-term growth potential. A standard recommendation for CEE and CIS countries in this position is to tighten fiscal policy, by increasing the rate of taxation or cutting government spending or both, as a way of reducing upward pressure on local interest and the exchange rates.

---

[20] Dolan (2012).
[21] Reuters (2013).

Third is to combine an independent monetary policy with a fixed exchange rate by closing the capital account through capital controls. Such controls may sometimes be a useful temporary expedient, but they are not unproblematic, especially in the longer term.

Figure 4.5 lists some of the main types of capital controls and some evidence on their varying effectiveness. Foreign exchange taxes can be, to some extent, effective in reducing the volume of flows in the short term, and can alter the composition of flows toward longer-term maturities. Unremunerated reserve requirements can also be effective in lengthening the maturity structure of inflows, but their effectiveness diminishes over time. There is some evidence that prudential measures that include some form of capital control, such as a limit on bank external borrowing, may be effective in reducing the volume of capital inflows.

Inflation Controls

Inflation, a rise in the overall level of prices, which erodes savings, lowers purchasing power, discourages investment, inhibits growth, fuels capital outflow, and, in extreme cases, provokes social and political unrest. People view it negatively and governments consequently have tried to battle inflation by adopting conservative and sustainable fiscal and monetary policies.

All economies that made the transition from the Soviet-style centralized-administrative model to a market economy in the early-1990s experienced significant inflation. The peak inflation rate for countries in the short-lived ruble area exceeded 1,000 percent. Poland's inflation, which peaked at over 500 percent in 1990, was the highest among transition economies outside the ruble area.[22] To bring inflation under control, Poland, like several other transition economies in the CEE, turned to a fixed exchange rate. Unlike the neighboring Baltic states, however, Poland did not institutionalize the fixed rate through a currency board or similar arrangement. With neither a strong institutional framework nor large foreign currency reserves, its fixed-rate disinflation strategy lacked credibility.

---

[22] Dolan (2012).

Types of capital controls	Volume of inflows	Composition of inflows
Foreign exchange tax	Can somewhat reduce the volume in the short term.	Can alter the composition of inflows toward longer-term maturities.
Unremunerated reserve requirements (URRs): Typically accompanied by other measures		Have been effectively applied reducing short-term inflows in overall inflows, but their effect diminishes over time.
Prudential measures with an element of capital control	Some evidence that prudential type controls can be effective in reducing capital inflows.	
Administrative controls: These are sometimes used in conjunction with URRs	Effectiveness depends largely on existence of other controls in the country.	

Figure 4.5 Effectiveness of capital control measures[23]

---

[23] IMF (2010a).

Macroeconomic trends have increasingly diverged across Central, Eastern, and Southeastern Europe (CESEE). While domestic demand is starting to recover in most countries helped by rising consumption and still accommodative global financial conditions, overall growth continues to disappoint and is slowing everywhere except the CEE region. Inflation paths have also diverged. Declining world food and energy prices and disinflationary spillovers from the euro area have put inflation on a downtrend across most of the region except Turkey, Russia, and the rest of the CIS, where high domestic food prices and exchange rate depreciation have kept inflation high.[24]

Growth has become increasingly divergent across CESEE countries from 2014 to 2015, slowing everywhere except in the CEE and the Baltics, as shown in Figures 4.6 and 4.7.

Russia and other CIS economies, for instance, have been affected by deepening geopolitical tensions surrounding eastern Ukraine and related sanctions and counter-sanctions. Russia's growth weakened in 2014 on account of contracting investment, declining real household income, and an increase in capital outflows. This same economic dynamics have been true for the meager growth in the Southeastern Europe (SEE) and Turkey, which has also decelerated due to country-specific factors. Also, floods hit

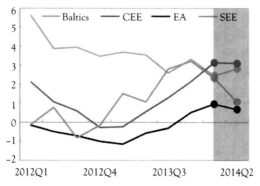

Figure 4.6 Quarterly GDP growth, 2012:Q1–2014:Q2, the Baltics, CEE, Euro Area, and SEE (percent, year-over-year)

Source: Haver Analytics; and IMF staff calculations.

---

[24] IMF (2014).

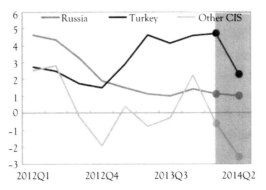

Figure 4.7   Quarterly GDP growth, 2012:Q1–2014:Q2, Other CIS, Russia, and Turkey (percent, year-over-year)

Source: Haver Analytics; and IMF staff calculations.

the SEE countries, contributing to the slowdown in growth. In Turkey, despite stronger net exports, faltering private investments following previous policy tightening has caused growth to slow in 2014 as well. In contrast, however, activities accelerated further in the CEE region, which has benefited from a pick up in FDI inflows, falling unemployment, and higher public spending in Hungary. In the Baltic region, growth was supported by favorable labor market conditions.

Inflation paths have, concurrently, continued to diverge as well, with inflation falling across most of the region, while picking up in Turkey, Russia, and other CIS countries. Declining world food and energy prices and low imported inflation from the euro area have continued to pull down prices in the CEE, SEE, and Baltic regions. In contrast, however, high domestic food prices, inflation expectations, and exchange-rate depreciations have kept inflation persistently high in Russia and other CIS countries, as well as Turkey. The recent ban on food imports in 2014 added to the upward pressure on prices in Russia while in Turkey, lax monetary policy has contributed as well.[25]

Of major concern, however, is the fact non-euro-area EU countries are importing low inflation from the euro area, causing countries pegged to the euro to be more exposed than those countries adopting inflation

---

[25] IMF (2014).

targeting. Still, however, we believe the major deflation drivers in the region are the falling world food and energy prices, as well as related administered prices.

Inflation has actually been falling sharply across Europe since 2012, with current inflation being well below the ECB's price stability objective in the euro area and in the CESEE and EU inflation targets, while a number of CESEE and EU euro peggers are experiencing outright deflation.[26] Across the CEE, inflation expectations have also drifted down, especially among those countries who peg their currencies to the euro, such as Bulgaria, Croatia, and Lithuania, which have since adopted the euro on January 1, 2015, but also in those countries that target their inflation rates, such as Czech Republic, Hungary, Poland, and Romania. At the same time, according to IMF, core inflation in the euro area and CESEE and EU countries, euro peggers, and inflation targeters has decoupled from developments in the rest of the world since the end of 2012.[27]

Inflation Targeting

As discussed in the previous section, the ongoing, synchronized disinflation across Europe raises the question of whether non-Eurozone EU countries are affected by the undershooting of the Eurozone inflation target, by other global factors, or by synchronized domestic, real sector developments. As argued by Plamen Iossifov,[28] Senior Economist in the European Department of IMF, the falling world food and energy prices have been the main disinflationary driver. However, countries, with more rigid exchange-rate regimes or higher shares of foreign value added in domestic demand or both, have also been affected by disinflationary spillovers from the Eurozone.

---

[26] Inflation-targeting CESEE/EU countries are the Czech Republic, Hungary, Poland, and Romania, while euro peggers includes Bulgaria, Croatia and Lithuania.

[27] Inflation-targeting CESEE/EU countries are the Czech Republic, Hungary, Poland, and Romania, while euro peggers includes Bulgaria, Croatia, and Lithuania.

[28] Iossifov (2015).

The recent drop in world food and oil prices, and where relevant cuts in administered prices of energy, has reignited the debate about good versus bad disinflation due to the fact these events have been an important driver of disinflation across EU countries outside the Eurozone.[29]

Furthermore, as argued by Iossifov,[30] core inflation, the overall inflation excluding volatile food and energy prices, has also drifted down, tracing price trends in the Eurozone, and increasingly diverging from developments in the rest of the world. This suggests possible disinflationary spillovers from the Eurozone to other EU countries, in light of their close trade links.

Overall, as argued by Iossifov,[31] the fall in oil prices will likely boost growth in the short run. But, it poses challenges to monetary policymaking, which focuses on medium-term risks. A prolonged undershooting of the inflation objective could damage central banks' credibility, which would make it much harder to escape the deflation trap.

Countries that peg to the euro do not have independent monetary policies and would have to rely on the ECB's QE policy response to persistently low inflation in the Eurozone. Where fiscal space allows, countries could also use discretionary, expansionary fiscal policies. Meanwhile, inflation-targeting central banks strive to keep inflation close to target over the medium term. Consequently, when faced with renewed disinflationary pressures, Iossifov[32] recommends they aim at targeting inflation closer to its goal, by stamping out "second-round" disinflationary effects of falling energy prices.

However, this could be challenging. With policy instruments at historical lows or at the zero lower bound, further easing by inflation-targeting central banks would need to weigh the benefits of normalizing price pressures with potential concerns about the impact on financial stability and capital flows and hence exchange rates. Easing monetary policy too much may prompt capital outflows, and while this may help depreciate exchange rates and raise inflation, there is always a risk that the process

---

[29] Moghadam, Teja, and Berkmen (2014).
[30] Iossifov (2015).
[31] Iossifov (2015).
[32] Iossifov (2015).

may go too far. This is of particular concern for countries with a high share of debt in foreign currencies, which are more exposed to changes in investors' risk appetite, geopolitical concerns, and global financing conditions.

Because interest rates and inflation rates tend to move in opposite directions, central bankers have adopted "inflation targeting" to control the general rise in the price level based on such understanding of the links from the monetary policy instruments of interest rates to inflation. By applying inflation targeting, a central bank estimates and makes public a projected, or "target," inflation rate and then attempts to use interest rate changes to steer actual inflation toward that target. Through such "transmission mechanism," the likely actions of a central bank will take to rise or lower interest rates become more transparent, which leads to increase of economic stability.

Inflation targeting, as a monetary-policy strategy, was introduced in New Zealand in 1990. It has been very successful in stabilizing both inflation and the real economy. As of 2010, as shown in Figure 4.8, it has been adopted by almost 30 advanced and emerging economies, including some in the CEE region (highlighted).

Inflation targeting is characterized by (1) an announced numerical inflation target, (2) an implementation of monetary policy that gives a major role to an inflation forecast and has been called forecast targeting, and (3) a high degree of transparency and accountability.[33] A major advantage of inflation targeting is that it combines elements of both "rules" and "discretion" in monetary policy. This "constrained discretion" framework combines two distinct elements: a precise numerical target for inflation in the medium term and a response to economic shocks in the short term.[34]

In emerging markets, particularly transition economies, the inflation picture can be quite different than those found in advanced economies. With unemployment rates hovering around long-term averages, these economies tend to be operating near their full potential. The concern for CEE and CIS economies is about high inflation together with potential

---

[33] Svensson (2008).
[34] Jahan (2012).

Targeting inflation				
Country	Inflation targeting adoption date	Inflation rate at adoption date (%)	2010 end-of-year inflation (%)	Target inflation rate (%)
New Zealand	1990	3.30	4.03	1–3
Canada	1991	6.90	2.23	2 ± 1
United Kingdom	1992	4.00	3.39	2
Australia	1993	2.00	2.65	2–3
Sweden	1993	1.80	2.10	2
Czech Republic	1997	6.80	2.00	3 ± 1
Israel	1997	8.10	2.62	2 ± 1
Poland	1998	10.60	3.10	2.5 ± 1
Brazil	1999	3.30	5.91	4.5 ± 1
Chile	1999	3.20	2.97	3 ± 1
Colombia	1999	9.30	3.17	2–4
S. Africa	2000	2.60	3.50	3–6
Thailand	2000	0.80	3.05	0.5–3
Hungary	2001	10.80	4.20	3 ± 1
Mexico	2001	9.00	4.40	3 ± 1
Iceland	2001	4.10	2.37	2.5 ± 1.5
S. Korea	2001	2.90	3.51	3 ± 1
Norway	2001	3.60	2.76	2.5 ± 1
Peru	2002	–0.10	2.08	2 ± 1
Philippines	2002	4.50	3.00	4 ± 1
Guatemala	2005	9.20	5.39	5 ± 1
Indonesia	2005	7.40	6.96	5 ± 1
Romania	2005	9.30	8.00	3 ± 1
Serbia	2006	10.80	10.29	4–8
Turkey	2006	7.70	6.40	5.5 ± 2
Armenia	2006	5.20	9.35	4.5 ± 1.5
Ghana	2007	10.50	8.58	8.5 ± 2
Albania	2009	3.70	3.40	3 ± 1

Figure 4.8 Summary of central banks using inflation targeting to control inflation

Sources: Hammond (2011); Roger (2010); and IMF staff calculations.

slower growth. Inflation has started to pick up in emerging markets during 2013, even as growth has fallen short of expectations, and looks particularly disappointing when compared with figures from before the 2008 financial crisis. A poorer growth-inflation trade-off suggests that economic potential in emerging markets has slowed considerably. This observation is a particular worry in the largest emerging markets, including China, India, and Brazil. All have been growing at poor rates compared with previous years, but in none has inflation fallen significantly during the past year.

Inflation targeting has been successfully practiced in a growing number of countries over the past 20 years, and many more countries are moving toward this framework. Although inflation targeting has proven to be a flexible framework that has been resilient in changing circumstances including during the recent global financial crisis, emerging markets however, must assess their economies to determine whether inflation targeting is appropriate for them or if it can be tailored to suit their needs. Facing the unique challenge of high inflation with slow growth, emerging economies may include currency rate and other alternatives, along with interest rates, to play a more pivotal role in stabilizing inflation.

CHAPTER 5

Challenges for Entering Eastern European Markets

Overview

As the developed Western economies still try to recover fully from the global financial crisis, Eastern Europe, a part of the world often neglected by investors and business leaders, has been showing impressive growth and maturity, both economically and politically. Stock markets in Bulgaria and Romania, for example, have appreciated significantly over the past year, and improving infrastructure coupled with still relatively cheap labor provide an attractive environment for investments in the manufacturing and service sectors.

Recent political unrest in some countries of the region, however, threatens to stymie economic progress and has reminded investors of the inherent risk that such high-return opportunities tend to carry, along with other factors discussed in this chapter, which should be seriously considered.

Even when bound by the ideology and strong embrace of the Soviet Union, Eastern Europe's countries differ widely, both economically and culturally. Additionally, as discussed throughout this book, the former Union of Soviet Socialist Republic's varying levels of economic commitment to each country, mostly born out of different strategic priorities, led to uneven infrastructure investments and industrial development. Even today, this developmental disparity is still evident.

Another important factor is the historical and cultural perspective that each country and its people possess. An investor would be well advised to seek trusted, and if possible local, advisers with a keen understanding of each country's culture and history. Failure to grasp local customs can be a pitfall when investing in any part of the world, but one would be hard pressed to find a place where such knowledge is more important than Eastern Europe.

On the political side, newly elevated activists supported by democracy-hungry populations, along with some freshly repainted old-regime politicians, dominated the initial scrambles for power in these countries. After the early victories by the new but inexperienced leaders, however, the former communist figures, well groomed for political survival through the decades, have emerged as major players in many of these countries.

In addition, despite their relative stability and impressive growth, the global financial crisis that started in 2007 continues to ripple through these countries, and their ongoing struggle to adapt to new ways of doing business still bears watching, as does the potential for renewed political turmoil. In our experience teaching this topic, consulting for several multinational corporations (MNC) around the world, and being a practitioner ourselves, we find that Eastern European markets are not easy to enter, despite the many government incentives already discussed throughout this book. Hence, entering these markets can be a complex endeavor, but the rewards can be immense as well.

In some countries, government interference, backward infrastructure, political instability, works' skill mismatch, and even lack of skilled workers, requires a lot of patience, perseverance, and specialized assistance. Opportunities in Eastern Europe markets, therefore, come with their own set of challenges.

Emerging economies, in particular these Eastern European transition economies, have also experienced large-scale structural change, in their case from the agricultural to the industrial sector. They are also often characterized by strong growth of the public sector, leading to a high share of employment in public activities often under the *clientelistic* control of ruling parties; a strong growth of informal sector; and a rapid demographic transition leading to a rapidly expanding and youthful population.

The modern urban sector employs relatively skilled labor, which attracts rural migrants with inadequate skills in search of higher wages, which leads to an oversupply of unskilled workers. The demographic transition leads to large numbers of young educated people in the labor market and high youth unemployment and consequently results in an oversupply of people with secondary education and skills. In addition, emigration of skilled workers (also known as *brain drain*) reduces the supply of skilled workers in the domestic economy, which typically also leads to shortages of highly skilled people.

The role of the state in these economies can be an important determinant of appropriate matching of skills supply and demand. Take South Korea, Singapore, and Taiwan, for example, which joined-up policymaking-enabled developmental states to anticipate future skills needs since the state was also involved in the very industrial policies, which generated the demand for skilled labor.[1]

Yet, although the integration of economic and skill formation policies in South Korea and Taiwan through modified forms of state planning was initially relatively successful, the power of the state to compel employers to train their workers gradually waned.[2] The state-directed policy eventually came under pressure to reform although the state retains a role in steering these economies. Kuruvilla et al.[3] argued that Singapore's successful national skills development model has the potential to move constantly toward higher skills equilibrium, but they question the long-term sustainability of the model and whether it is transferable to other developing countries. Recent research by Özsagir et al.[4] has shown a positive relationship between the extent of vocational training and the index of industrial production.

Skill Mismatches

Skill mismatches and skill shortages have become a priority concern for policymakers in many countries, especially since the onset of the global economic crisis and its intensification through the crisis in the Eurozone. Endogenous growth models emphasize that human capital is a key resource for growth. In fact, skill mismatch has an adverse effect on the efficiency of labor markets, particularly in transition economies, raising unemployment above the levels that could potentially be achieved given

---

[1] Green et al. (1999a).
[2] Green et al. (1999b).
[3] Kuruvilla, Erickson, and Hwang (2002).
[4] Özsagir and Bayraktutan (2010).

the level of aggregate demand. Efficient matching would reduce frictional and structural unemployment and ensure that vacancies are matched to workers with appropriate qualifications and skills.[5]

For instance, often the lack of specialized education of the workforce translates into thwarted growth being curbed by the lack of a skilled workforce. According to models of endogenous growth, the skill levels of the workforce, particularly in transition economies, are an important driver of economic development. This is partly due to different patterns of structural change and partly associated with demographic factors. Countries with high population growth rates may experience oversupply of educated school leavers; countries with falling populations may experience undersupply of both skilled and unskilled workers. There is also evidence of gender-biased mismatch in these markets. Among the main challenges to the development of an effective skill matching system, and the corresponding policy design for transition countries, are weak capacities of government institutions including the employment services, underfunding of state provided training services, slow reforms of the education systems, and low level of in-house training by employers.

Most Eastern European countries have experienced volatile labor markets for many years. Although unemployment rates were on a falling trend up to 2008, long-term unemployment has been persistently high in many countries, as shown in Table 5.1, leading to a corresponding obsolescence of skills among a large section of the workforce. After almost a decade of sustained economic growth, the global economic crisis brought about an abrupt reversal of fortunes and began to increase in most countries of the region.[6] Long-term unemployment in the region is a serious problem, especially affecting older workers with obsolete skills. Youth unemployment is generally high[7] particularly in countries with a rapidly growing population. On the demand side of the labor market, many old large-scale industries declined or closed down, while most new jobs emerged in the service industries among which a range of new skills

---

[5] Petrolongo and Pissarides (2001).
[6] ETF (2011, 27).
[7] Kolev and Saget (2005).

Table 5.1 Unemployment rates for Eastern European countries

Country	Unemployment rate	Last updated	Previous %	Highest %	Lowest %
Albania	17.5	Sep, 2015	17.3	22.3	12.1
Bosnia and Herzegovina	42.81	Oct, 2015	42.97	46.1	39.03
Bulgaria	9.9	Nov, 2015	9.5	19.27	4.68
Croatia	17.7	Nov, 2015	17.2	23.6	12.2
Czech Republic	5.9	Nov, 2015	5.9	9.69	0.09
Estonia	5.2	Sep, 2015	6.5	20.1	0.5
Hungary	6.2	Nov, 2015	6.4	11.8	5.5
Kosovo	35.3	Dec, 2014	30	57	30
Latvia	9.7	Sep, 2015	9.8	20.7	5.4
Lithuania	8.4	Nov, 2015	8.3	15.3	2.7
Macedonia	25.48	Sep, 2015	26.84	37.3	25.48
Montenegro	16.35	Nov, 2015	15.67	31	10.2
Poland	9.6	Nov, 2015	9.6	20.7	0.3
Romania	6.7	Nov, 2015	6.8	8.1	5.4
Serbia	17.3	Sep, 2015	17.9	25.5	13.3
Slovakia	10.8	Nov, 2015	11	19.79	7.36
Slovenia	11.7	Oct, 2015	11.5	15.5	6.3

Source: tradingeconomics.com

are needed.[8] Regional mismatch also emerged as a specific problem due to the collapse of industries in peripheral areas and mono-industrial towns.[9]

Education System

Education systems in many transition countries are still character-ized by poor quality and irrelevance of much education provision in the region.[10] It is increasingly been recognized that curricula inherited

---

[8] Bartlett (2007).

[9] Bornhorst and Commander (2006); Newell and Pastore (2006).

[10] Sondergaard and Murthi (2012).

from the previous communist system were unsuited to the development
of a service-oriented post-Fordist[11] market economy and have not been
upgraded sufficiently to reflect the new occupations that have emerged in
the service sectors and in high technology industries. Skills that are taught
in vocational education institutions tend to be too specialized in obsolete
occupations. Education methods are often outdated and dependent on
rote learning, based on memorization techniques and repetition rather
than problem solving. There is generally a deficit of education in transferable skills (so-called "soft skills").

Skills produced by the education system are often no longer demanded
in the labor market. A recent study of the development of skills mismatches in Eastern Europe found that "even when people hold the correct
qualification for an occupation they may not necessarily have the skills
needed to effectively perform the job and satisfy employer expectations.
Rapid technological and economic change makes it difficult to predict
what types of skills will be needed in the near and more distant future
and what kinds of new jobs will appear."[12] Moreover, because of structural
change, it seems that skill mismatch is a more permanent phenomenon
in Eastern European markets than in the advanced economies resulting
in high levels of long-term unemployment, and that skills mismatch
increases with the age of workers, rather than falling as it does in the
developed economies.

Economic Restructuring

Skill shortages and surpluses of various types are a challenge for Eastern
European countries as a consequence of economic restructuring. The
process of economic transition involved a simultaneous process of job
destruction and job creation in which unskilled workers lost employment
disproportionately as the skill content of blue-collar work increased due

---

[11] Post-Fordism is the name given by some scholars to what they describe as
the dominant system of economic production, consumption and associated
socio-economic phenomena, in most industrialized countries since the late 20th
century.

[12] ETF (2011, 229).

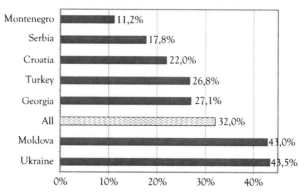

Figure 5.1 Proportion of firms reporting that an inadequately educated workforce is a "major or very severe" obstacle to the firm (%)

Source: BEEPS Survey (2010), European Bank for Reconstruction and Development (EBRD).

to technological change. Newly created jobs typically require different types of skills to those that have been destroyed. This process of restructuring and the expansion of demand for new skills has often taken place more rapidly than the education and training systems have been able to adept, leading to skill shortages. Figure 5.1 provides a sample of a handful of Eastern Europeans countries, depicting the proportion of business organizations reporting that an inadequately educated workforce is *a major or very severe* obstacle to the firm, in percentages points.

Legal Framework and Trading Policies

Other challenges that arise are legal frameworks with regard to trade policies, which may be absent or underdeveloped, or tendencies for political paternalism or blatant interferences, especially in those countries that have not yet joined the European Union (EU), such as Albania, Armenia, Belarus, Bosnia and Herzegovina, Kosovo, Macedonia, to name a few.

All EU countries, for example, do not recognize Kosovo's independence, although a surprise Serbia-Kosovo deal, brokered by EU High Representative Catherine Ashton in 2013, paves the way for its eventual EU membership. The other Western Balkan countries have all been told they can one day follow Croatia into the EU, as long as they make progress on democratic and economic reforms. Moving closer toward the EU implies meeting the criteria and conditions for each stage. These relate to the Copenhagen membership criteria[13] and the stabilization and association process,[14] including on regional cooperation, good neighborly relations, and full cooperation with the International Criminal Tribunal for the former Yugoslavia. The Western Balkan countries need to effectively address the priorities set out in their accession or European partnerships. The pace of each country's progress is determined by its own achievements in this respect.

As for most industrialized countries, trade volumes increased significantly after World War II, but trade has been identified as one potential culprit for the worsened position of low-skilled workers.[15] Trade is thought to have affected the demand for low-skilled workers in two ways. It is thought to have reduced the relative demand for low-skilled labor and to have made the demand more responsive to changes in the price of low-skilled labor. Both effects would reduce the relative wages of low-skilled workers in economies with flexible labor markets. In economies where labor market rigidities prevent wages from falling, an increased relative unemployment rate of low-skilled labor may result. Country-specific labor market characteristics would thus have an important effect on whether and to which extent relative wages or trade or both affect the relative unemployment rates.

With strong increases in skill inequalities over the 1980s and part of the 1990s and continuing integration of economies around the world, trading in emerging markets, particularly in Eastern Europe faced major

---

[13] The Copenhagen criteria are the rules that define whether a country is eligible to join the European Union. The criteria require that a state has the institutions to preserve democratic governance and human rights, has a functioning market economy, and accepts the obligations and intent of the EU.

[14] In talks with countries that have expressed a wish to join the European Union, the EU typically concludes Association Agreements in exchange for commitments to political, economic, trade, or human rights reform in that country. In exchange, the country may be offered tariff-free access to some or all EU markets (industrial goods, agricultural products, etc.), and financial or technical assistance.

[15] Other factors that affect wage and employment inequalities are migration, technological change and changes in the skill distribution of the labor force.

challenges and imbalances. Whilesome markets were very well developed and worker's skills were high, other markets in the region lacked both. We'd argue that there is potentially negative effect of trade with developing countries in Eastern Europe on low-skilled workers in industrialized countries.

Public administration in Eastern European economies has much to be desired, although overall it ranks much better than the Brazil, Russia, India, China, and South Africa (BRICS) and other leading emerging market blocs. The 2015' *Doing Business*[16] study by the World Bank, which rank economies on their ease of doing business on a scale of 1 to 189, where a high ease of doing business ranking means the regulatory environment is more conducive to the starting and operation of a local firm is very telling.[17] As depicted in Table 5.2, the study ranks Macedonia 12th, Lithuania 20th, and Latvia 22nd as the easiest countries of doing business

Table 5.2 Ascending list of most ease of doing business countries in Europe and Central Asia

Economy	Ease of doing business rank
Macedonia, FYR	12
Lithuania	20
Latvia	22
Georgia	24
Armenia	35
Romania	37
Bulgaria	38
Croatia	40
Kazakhstan	41
Belarus	44
Montenegro	46
Cyprus	47

(*Continued*)

---

[16] The World Bank (2015).

[17] The rankings are determined by sorting the aggregate distance to frontier scores on 10 topics, each consisting of several indicators, giving equal weight to each topic. The rankings for all economies are benchmarked to June 2015.

Table 5.2 Ascending list of most ease of doing business countries in Europe and Central Asia (Continued)

Economy	Ease of doing business rank
Russian Federation	51
Moldova	52
Turkey	55
Serbia	59
Azerbaijan	63
Kosovo	66
Kyrgyz Republic	67
Bosnia and Herzegovina	79
Ukraine	83
Uzbekistan	87
Albania	97
Tajikistan	132

Source: World Bank (2015).

in Europe and Central Asia, out of 189 countries, while ranking Kosovo 66th, Bosnia and Herzegovina 79th, and Albania 97th. The discrepancy between the first three and the last ones are remarkable. By comparison, the study ranks Brazil 116th, Russia 51st, India 130th, China 84th, and South Africa 73rd, respectively out of 189 countries.

Does all this mean that foreign investors should avoid trading with or investing in Eastern Europe markets? On the contrary, however, any organized program of opening up to Eastern Europe markets must include specialized expertise, on-the-ground knowledge, local partnerships, and, most of all, patience.

Why Multinationals Fail in Eastern Europe Markets

Pacek and Thorniley[18] identified an exhaustive range of factors contributing to the failure of companies from advanced economies into Eastern

---

[18] Pacek and Thorniley (2007).

Europe markets. These factors may be divided into external and internal factors and almost all are related to strategic and leadership issues:

- Leaders fail to consider Eastern Europe markets as an integral part of strategy and acknowledge that such markets need to be approached with a distinct set of criteria for judging progress and success.
- Top leaders fail to commit sufficient resources to get businesses established and grown in Eastern Europe markets, or acknowledge that it is never a short-term affair.
- MNCs fail to appoint a head manager for Eastern Europe markets and often assign this responsibility to an international manager who is responsible for markets in both advanced and emerging markets. The problem with this is that operational approaches are distinct in each of these markets, as evidenced on Table 5.3.
- MNCs fail to understand that business is driven by heads of regions and business units rather than by heads of functional areas. While the former has a focus and appreciation for the Eastern Europe economies, the latter tends also to be interested in advanced markets.
- MNCs do not acknowledge that Eastern Europe markets operate under distinct business models and structures, and often merely transfer practices tested in advanced economies without considering adaptation.
- The board members of many MNCs have limited diversity in terms of culture and ethnic background and do not develop sufficient appreciation for the peculiarities of the Eastern Europe markets.
- MNCs underestimate the potential and often early competition from smaller international and domestic companies, thus never accepting that they may be destined as a follower in Eastern Europe markets.
- Economic and political crisis also exist in Eastern European markets, as discussed earlier, and have a significant impact on business performance. Top managers need to understand this,

be prepared to adapt and introduce new tactics rather than changing strategy, which despite having short-term success, tends to be the wrong approach in the long term.

- MNCs get alarmed by short-term slippages and cut costs to attain favorable temporary results, yet this is likely to have a structural impact on strategy implementation and long-term results.

- MNCs set unrealistic targets to achieve, which leave managers with limited maneuvering space and short-lived careers.

- MNCs fail to recognize that entering the market early is fundamental in establishing networks, developing brands, and learning the larger context from which it will operate.

- Senior leaders fail to recognize that developing a network of reliable contacts often requires establishing friendships with locals, which requires time and visibility in Eastern European markets.

- MNCs fail to empower regional and country managers and delegate decision-making power to local managers.

- Foreign companies fail to recognize that Eastern European markets are more price-sensitive and often stick to their pricing structures instead of adapting to local sensitivities.

- International firms fail to recognize that their product portfolio is not tailored to the lower and middle segments of emergent markets and do not develop innovations that are context-oriented.

- Foreign companies underestimate the competition from local companies in emergent markets, which gradually move up from lower to upper segments. Local companies understand better than anyone about local markets, sometimes employ dubious practices, and often have the support of local governments.

- One of the largest obstacles that foreign companies face may be the unwillingness to change long-standing business practices.

- Another challenge is to appoint senior managers who are not familiar with the local market, culture, and language in emerging countries.

- The fact that demand is volatile and unpredictable in emerging and frontier markets may discourage multinationals, which often expect reliable market information.

The failure factors are numerous and diverse but as Pacek and Thorniley noted, it all boils down to a lack of adequate market entry preparation. Preparation requires companies to continuously research the external environment and know how to use internal resources to take advantage of opportunities. Hence, a preliminary audit that focuses on external and internal factors is essential. The external factors may be examined by posing questions concerning the market, the political environment, the economic environment, and the business environment, as depicted in Table 5.3.

Table 5.3 External factors and sample questions

Understanding the market	
Market potential	• How large and wealthy is the market? • Is there an unsatisfied demand for the product or service?
Understanding local consumers or customers	• Who are the consumers and customers? What are their characteristics? • How do consumers make their decisions?
Reaching the consumer or customer	• How difficult or easy is it to reach potential consumers or customers? • How do competitors and noncompetitors reach their customers?
Competition	• Which competitors are already operating in the market? • How strong are these competitors?
Lessons learned by noncompetitors	• What do noncompetitors say about the business environment in the country? • What have been the largest obstacles to successful operations?
Local culture	• What aspects of local culture are relevant to running a successful local business?
Understanding the political and economic environment	
Economic outlook	• How sustainable is economic growth? • What is driving economic growth?
Political outlook	• What is the level of political risk and how will or might it affect the business?

(Continued)

Table 5.3 External factors and sample questions (Continued)

Government policies	• Does the government allow a level playing field? • Is the government in the hands of local lobbies?
Understanding the business environment	
Finance	• Is it possible to finance operations locally? • What access do customers or consumers have to finance?
Labor market	• What are the wage or salary rates for the employees who will be needed? • What are the most effective ways of recruiting local employees?
Taxation	• What are the current levels of taxation? • What is the outlook for tax incentives?
Legal environment	• How effective and efficient is the local judiciary? • Is there any hope that the legal system will improve?
Bureaucratic obstacles to business	• What are the most common bureaucratic obstacles for business? • How easy or difficult it is to set up business in the country?
Crime and corruption	• Is crime a problem for business? • What is the level of corruption?
Infrastructure	• What is the quality of local transport infrastructure? • And telecommunications?
Foreign trade environment	• Is the country a World Trade Organization (WTO) member? • Does it belong to any trading blocs or regional free-trade areas?
Cost of building a business and brand	• How expensive is it to build a brand? • How much time will it take to do what is necessary to get the business off the ground?

By the same token, the internal factors must inquire about resources, products, organization, and risks, as depicted in Table 5.4.

Having done a preliminary external and internal audit, managers need to prepare a business proposal describing what to do, how to do it, by when, and resources required. Businesses must then ask themselves whether there are similar or better opportunities available in other Eastern Europe markets. How then, can we compare the potential of different Eastern Europe markets?

Table 5.4 Internal factors and sample questions

Resources	• How much time and money will be required? • Is the CEO committed to support business development and provide necessary resources? And the senior managers? • What human resources are needed?
Products	• Is the product portfolio right for the market? • Will investment be available for developing new products?
Organization	• Could existing internal processes and operational practices help or hinder what is planned? • What existing capabilities can be drawn?
Risks	• Can the risks that have been identified be managed? • How would entry be financed?

Ranking Eastern European Markets

According to the GlobalEdge[19] team at the International Business Center at The Eli Broad Graduate School of Management, Michigan State University, there are three main reasons why Eastern European markets are attractive. They are target markets, manufacturing bases, and sourcing destinations.

As manufacturing bases they present advantages such as low-wages, high-quality labor for manufacturing and assembly operations. Slovakia has been the world's largest producer of cars per capita with currently three automobile assembly plants in the country, including Volkswagen's in Bratislava, PSA Peugeot Citroën's in Trnava, and Kia Motors' Žilina Plant, and by 2018, Jaguar Land Rover is set to open the country's fourth automobile assembly plant in Nitra.[20] The Czech Republic's long and rich scientific traditions, with research based on cooperation between universities, the Academy of Sciences of the Czech Republic, and other specialized research centers often bring new inventions and contributions to market, including but not limited to the modern contact lens, the separation of modern blood types, and the production of Semtex plastic explosive. Several MNCs are already present in Lithuania, including PricewaterhouseCoopers, Ernst & Young, Societe Generale, UniCredit,

---

[19] Based on GlobalEdge. http://globaledge.msu.edu/mpi
[20] Pitas (2015).

Thermo Fisher Scientific, Phillip Morris, Kraft Foods, Mars, Marks & Spencer, GlaxoSmithKline, United Colors of Benetton, Deichmann, Statoil, Neste Oil, Lukoil, Tele2, Hesburger, and Modern Times Group.

From Indicators to Institutions

It is common wisdom that size and growth potential are the two best criteria to select an Eastern Europe market. Not so for Khanna and Palepu[21] who argue that lack of institutions, such as distribution systems, credit cards systems, or data research firms, is the primary factor to consider when entering into an emerging market, and the Eastern European markets are no different. For them, the fact that Eastern Europe markets have poor institutions, thus, inefficient business operations, present the best business opportunities for companies operating in such dynamic markets. However, the ways businesses enter into Eastern European markets are different, and are contingent upon variations presented by the institutions and the abilities of the firms.

Khanna and Palepu point out that the use of composite indexes to assess the potential of emerging markets, as executives often do, has limited use in Eastern European markets because these indicators do not capture the soft infrastructures and institutions. These composite indexes are useful in ranking market potential of countries when and only these countries have similar institutional environments. When soft infrastructures differ, we must then look at the institutional context in each market.

Best Opportunities Fill in Institutional Voids

From an institutional viewpoint the market is a transactional place embedded in information and property rights, and Eastern European markets are a place where one or both of these features are underdeveloped.[22] Most definitions of Eastern European markets are descriptive, often based on poverty and growth indicators, and their categoric *stage* as a transition economy. In contrast, a structural definition as proposed

---

[21] Khanna and Palepu (2010).
[22] Khanna and Palepu (2010).

by Khanna and Palepu points to issues which are problematic, therefore allowing an immediate identification of solutions. Moreover, a structural definition allows us not only to understand commonalities among Eastern European markets but also to understand what differentiates each of these markets. Finally a structural approach provides a more precise understanding of the market dynamics that genuinely differentiates Eastern Europe markets from advanced economies.

To illustrate, let us contrast the equity capital markets of South Korea and Chile. According to the International Finance Corporation definition, South Korea is not an emerging market because it is an Organization for Economic Cooperation and Development member; however, when we look at its equity capital market, we notice that until recently it was not functioning well, in other words it has an institutional void. Chile on the other hand is considered an emerging market in Latin America but it has an efficient capital market, thus no institutional void appears in this sector. However Chile has institutional voids in other markets such as the products market. Similar factors exist among Eastern European countries that are already members of the EU versus those that are not.

Strategy formulation in Eastern European markets, therefore, must begin with a map of institutional voids. What works in the headquarters of a multinational company does not per se work in new locations with different institutional environments. The most common mistake companies do when entering Eastern European markets is to overestimate the importance of past experience. This common error reflects a recency bias: a person assumes that recent successful experiences may be transferred to other places. A manager may incorrectly assume that the way people are motivated in one country would be the same in the new country (context). It may be assumed that everyone likes to be appreciated, but the way of expressing appreciation depends on the institutional environment. Khanna and Palepu point out that the human element is the cornerstone of operating in new contexts. Ultimately, human beings, who provide a mix of history, culture, and interactions, create institutions.

In short, based on Khanna and Palepu's institutional approach to Eastern European markets, it is necessary to answer several questions, including but not limited to:

- Which institutions are working and missing?
- Which parts of our business model (in the home country) would be affected by these voids?
- How can we build competitive advantage based on our ability to navigate institutional voids?
- How can we profit from the structural reality of Eastern European markets today by identifying opportunities to fill voids, serving as market intermediaries?

Strategies for Eastern European Markets

The work of Khanna and Palepu indicates that there are four generic strategic choices for companies operating in emerging markets, which also apply for Eastern European markets:

- Replicate or adapt?
- Compete alone or collaborate?
- Accept or attempt to change market context?
- Enter, wait, or exit?

Eastern European markets attract two competing types of firms, the developed market-based multinationals and the emerging market-based companies. Both bring different advantages to fill institutional voids. MNCs bring brands, capital talent, and resources, such as the case of several ones based in Lithuania, whereas local companies contribute with local contacts and context knowledge. Because they have different strengths and resources, foreign and domestic firms will compete differently and must develop strategies accordingly. Table 5.5 summarizes the strategies and options for both MNCs and local companies.

Anand P. Arkalgud[23] provides a good example of how companies fill institutional voids. Take the example of India where road infrastructure is still underdeveloped in terms of quality and connectivity. Traditionally Tata Motors has been the dominant player in the auto industry but when it started to receive competition from Volvo in the truck segment and

---

[23] Arkalgud (2011).

Table 5.5 *Responding to institutional voids*

Strategic choice	Options for multinationals from developed countries	Options for emerging market-based companies
Replicate or adapt?	• Replicate business model, exploiting relative advantage of global brand, credibility, know-how, talent, finance, and other factor inputs. • Adapt business models, products, or organizations to institutional voids.	• Copy business model from developed countries. • Exploit local knowledge, capabilities, and ability to navigate institutional voids to build tailored business models.
Compete alone or collaborate?	• Compete alone. • Acquire capabilities to navigate institutional voids through local partnerships or joint ventures (JVs).	• Compete alone. • Acquire capabilities from developed markets through partnerships or JVs with multinational companies to bypass institutional voids.
Accept or attempt to change market context?	• Take market context as given. • Fill institutional voids in service of own business.	• Take market context as given. • Fill institutional voids in service of own business.
Enter, wait, or exit?	• Enter or stay in market spite of institutional voids. • Emphasize opportunities elsewhere.	• Build business in home market in spite of institutional voids. • Exit home market early in corporate history if capabilities unrewarded at home.

Source: Khanna and Palepu (2010).

by Japanese automakers in the car segment, Tata responded. It created a mini-truck that not only provided more capacity and safety than the two- and three-wheeled pollutant vehicles used to access market areas but also an environmentally sound vehicle, one that could easily maneuver U-turns in such narrow streets.

Another case in India involved Coca Cola, which discovered that their beverages were being sold "warm." Coca Cola realized that it needed a solution to sell its product "chilled." The reason for the warm bottles was the fact that electricity supplies in these remote locations were unstable, especially in summer periods. Thus the company developed a solar-powered cooler and partnered with a local refrigeration company.

Tarun Khanna and Krishna Palepu propose the following five contexts as a framework in assessing the institutional environment of any country. The five contexts include the markets needed to acquire input (product, labor, and capital), and markets needed to sell output. This is referred to as the products and services market. In addition to these three dimensions the framework includes a broader sociopolitical context defined by political and social systems and degrees of openness. When applying the framework, managers need to ask a set of questions in each dimension. An example of these questions is indicated in Table 5.6.

Conclusion

Entry mode[24] is determined by product, market and organizational factors. In regard to products and services, MNCs need to know whether the nature and range of the product or service, along with available marketing strategies, will require any adaptation. If so, they should consider a partner in the Eastern European country they plan to enter. Usually a higher level of control and resource commitment in the foreign market is required for new or wider product offerings as well as higher levels of adaptation. When taking into account market factors, managers need to consider physical distance and experience, as well as identify appropriate marketing strategies and distribution channels, and priorities in revenues, costs and profits.

Organizationally, major concerns are communication with foreign operations and control of overseas activities. One particular concern in foreign markets is the control of assets. Firms will prefer to internalize activities where there is a higher chance of opportunism by the partners in those markets.

For Eastern Europe in particular, the region is poised for further growth, but some major obstacles remain on the road to prosperity. Chief

---

[24] http://globaledge.msu.edu/reference-desk/online-course-modules/market-research-and-entry

Table 5.6 Framework to assess institutional voids

Institutional dimension	Questions
Product markets	1. Can companies easily obtain reliable data on customer tastes and purchase behaviors? Are there cultural barriers to market research? Do world-class market research firms operate in the country?
	2. Can consumers easily obtain unbiased information on the quality of the goods and services they want to buy? Are there independent consumer organizations and publications that provide such information?
	3. Can companies access raw materials and components of good quality? Is there a deep network of suppliers? Are there firms that assess suppliers' quality and reliability? Can companies enforce contracts with suppliers?
	4. How strong are the logistics and transportation infrastructures? Have global logistics companies set up local operations?
	5. Do large retail chains exist in the country? If so, do they cover the entire country or only the major cities? Do they reach all consumers or only wealthy ones?
	6. Are there other types of distribution channels, such as direct-to-consumer channels and discount retail channels that deliver products to customers?
	7. Is it difficult for multinationals to collect receivables from local retailers?
	8. Do consumers use credit cards, or does cash dominate transactions? Can consumers get credit to make purchases? Are data on customer creditworthiness available?
	9. What recourse do consumers have against false claims by companies or defective products and services?
	10. How do companies deliver after-sales service to consumers? Is it possible to set up a nationwide service network? Are third-party service providers reliable?
	11. Are consumers willing to try new products and services? Do they trust goods from local companies? How about from foreign companies?
	12. What kind of product-related environmental and safety regulations are in place? How do the authorities enforce those regulations?

Institutional dimension	Questions
Labor markets	1. How strong is the country's education infrastructure, especially for technical and management training? Does it have a good elementary and secondary education system as well?
	2. Do people study and do business in English or in another international language, or do they mainly speak a local language?
	3. Are data available to help sort out the quality of the country's educational institutions?
	4. Can employees move easily from one company to another? Does the local culture support that movement? Do recruitment agencies facilitate executive mobility?
	5. What are the major postrecruitment-training needs of the people that multinationals hire locally?
	6. Is pay for performance a standard practice? How much weight do executives give seniority, as opposed to merit, in making promotion decisions?
	7. Would a company be able to enforce employment contracts with senior executives? Could it protect itself against executives who leave the firm and then compete against it? Could it stop employees from stealing trade secrets and intellectual property?
	8. Does the local culture accept foreign managers? Do the laws allow a firm to transfer locally hired people to another country? Do managers want to stay or leave the nation?
	9. How are the rights of workers protected? How strong are the country's trade unions? Do they defend workers' interests or only advance a political agenda?
	10. Can companies use stock options and stock-based compensation schemes to motivate employees?
	11. Do the laws and regulations limit a firm's ability to restructure, downsize, or shut down?
	12. If a company were to adopt its local rivals' or suppliers' business practices, such as the use of child labor, would that tarnish its image overseas?

Institutional dimension	Questions
Capital markets	1. How effective are the country's banks, insurance companies, and mutual funds at collecting savings and channeling them into investments?
	2. Are financial institutions managed well? Is their decision making transparent? Do noneconomic considerations, such as family ties, influence their investment decisions?
	3. Can companies raise large amounts of equity capital in the stock market? Is there a market for corporate debt?
	4. Does a venture capital industry exist? If so, does it allow individuals with good ideas to raise funds?
	5. How reliable are sources of information on company performance? Do the accounting standards and disclosure regulations permit investors and creditors to monitor company management?
	6. Do independent financial analysts, rating agencies, and the media offer unbiased information on companies?
	7. How effective are corporate governance norms and standards at protecting shareholder interests?
	8. Are corporate boards independent and empowered, and do they have independent directors?
	9. Are regulators effective at monitoring the banking industry and stock markets?
	10. How well do the courts deal with fraud?
	11. Do the laws permit companies to engage in hostile takeovers? Can shareholders organize themselves to remove entrenched managers through proxy fights?
	12. Is there an orderly bankruptcy process that balances the interests of owners, creditors, and other stakeholders?

Institutional dimension	Questions
Political and social system	1. To whom are the country's politicians accountable? Are there strong political groups that oppose the ruling party? Do elections take place regularly? 2. Are the roles of the legislative, executive, and judiciary clearly defined? What is the distribution of power between the central, state, and city governments? 3. Does the government go beyond regulating business to interfering in it or running companies? 4. Do the laws articulate and protect private property rights? 5. What is the quality of the country's bureaucrats? What are bureaucrats' incentives and career trajectories? 6. Is the judiciary independent? Do the courts adjudicate disputes and enforce contracts in a timely and impartial manner? How effective are the quasi-judicial regulatory institutions that set and enforce rules for business activities? 7. Do religious, linguistic, regional, and ethnic groups coexist peacefully, or are there tensions between them? 8. How vibrant and independent is the media? Are newspapers and magazines neutral, or do they represent sectarian interests? 9. Are nongovernmental organizations, civil rights groups, and environmental groups active in the country? 10. Do people tolerate corruption in business and government? 11. What role do family ties play in business? 12. Can strangers be trusted to honor a contract in the country?

Institutional dimension	Questions
Openness	1. Are the country's government, media, and people receptive to foreign investment? Do citizens trust companies and individuals from some parts of the world more than others?
	2. What restrictions does the government place on foreign investment? Are those restrictions in place to facilitate the growth of domestic companies, to protect state monopolies, or because people are suspicious of multinationals?
	3. Can a company make greenfield investments and acquire local companies, or can it only break into the market by entering into JV? Will that company be free to choose partners based purely on economic considerations?
	4. Does the country allow the presence of foreign intermediaries such as market research and advertising firms, retailers, media companies, banks, insurance companies, venture capital firms, auditing firms, management consulting firms, and educational institutions?
	5. How long does it take to start a new venture in the country? How cumbersome are the government's procedures for permitting the launch of a wholly foreign-owned business?
	6. Are there restrictions on portfolio investments by overseas companies or on dividend repatriation by multinationals?
	7. Does the market drive exchange rates, or does the government control them? If it's the latter, does the government try to maintain a stable exchange rate, or does it try to favor domestic products over imports by propping up the local currency?
	8. What would be the impact of tariffs on a company's capital goods and raw materials imports? How would import duties affect that company's ability to manufacture its products locally versus exporting them from home?
	9. Can a company set up its business anywhere in the country? If the government restricts the company's location choices, are its motives political, or is it inspired by a logical regional development strategy?
	10. Has the country signed free-trade agreements with other nations? If so, do those agreements favor investments by companies from some parts of the world over others?
	11. Does the government allow foreign executives to enter and leave the country freely? How difficult is it to get work permits for managers and engineers?
	12. Does the country allow its citizens to travel abroad freely? Can ideas flow into the country unrestricted? Are people permitted to debate and accept those ideas?

obstacles among them are social and economic tensions between ethnic groups, which can create problems ranging from labor markets conflicts to security risks for local businesses. Such dynamics are a special concern during periods of economic distress, high unemployment, and political unrest—known causes of nationalistic, antioutsider fervor.

The role of Russia is another concern. After the Soviet Union's fall, Eastern Europe began shifting its allegiances to the West. With Russia struggling through its own economic problems at the time, it seemed likely the realignment would endure. Today, trade with the West is up and several countries in the Eastern European region are members of North Atlantic Treaty Organization (NATO) and the European Union.

But Russia should not be underestimated. It still plays an important role in the economies of Eastern Europe. And Vladimir Putin has been frank about his ambition to create a Eurasian economic union, composed mainly of former Soviet states, as a counterweight to the EU. The long-term possibility of new realignments, this time toward the East, cannot be dismissed.

A case in point, most recently, the developments in Crimea have shown that despite years of change and effort toward global integration, Russian strategic goals in the region should not be overlooked. Putin's rule, reminiscent of the iron hands that governed Russia during the Soviet era, coupled with those weakened by the *Great Recession* in the West, is a recipe for a meal that's only served very cold.

Russia's annexation of Crimea, and even more importantly, the inability of the West to do much to prevent it, shows the complex political and economic relations in the region and the political, and military, power that Russia still holds. The brazen move by President Putin is a source of much anxiety in Eastern Europe, particularly by neighbors of the big superpower, Poland being one of them. Several of the Eastern European countries are NATO members, which eases a bit worries of invasion, but Russia remains a strong business partner to much of Europe and especially to countries from the former Eastern European bloc, and economic sanctions against Russia would surely be felt and have a lasting effect across the continent.

CHAPTER 6

Political Risk
in Eastern Europe

The decision of whether or not to invest in emerging markets should include an assessment of the political environment. Political discontinuities create a level of uncertainty for companies and individuals because they can lead to significant shifts in policies, regulations, governmental administration, and other potential risk factors that are not typically associated with advanced economies. Political instability can lead to restrictions on products, technology, and labor and even lead to practices of discrimination against foreign firms. This chapter will survey the impact of a series of political and economic risk assessments that include factors such as economic growth, labor unrest, social unrest, armed conflict, and how those elements interact with local investments and foreign-direct investment (FDI).

Table 6.1 provides data across a series of government indicators. Table 6.2 follows these indicators with a set of rankings of political risk for Central and Eastern Europe (CEE) countries and nearby states in the region based on Freedom House indices. Countries are rated on a scale of 1 to 7, with 1 representing the highest and 7 the lowest level of democratic progress. The average rating across the categories of "Electoral Process," "Civil Society," "Independent Media," "National Democratic Governance," "Local Democratic Governance," "Judicial Framework and Independence," and "Corruption" are average to create the overall country score. Each ranking is calculated using a series of variables derived from the most recent political data available (as of December 2014).

The reader might wonder why assess democratic governance in relation to political risk. A new field in political science has emerged which attempts to explore greater connections between these two phenomena.

Table 6.1 Country comparisons of select government indicators

Country	Total tax rate (% of commercial profits)	Proportion of seats held by women in national parliaments (%)	Population growth (annual %)	Public spending on education, total (% of GDP)	Literacy rate, (% of people aged 15 and above)
Bosnia and Herzegovina	23.3	21.4	-0.12	-	98.153
Bulgaria	27.0	24.6	-0.56	4.097	98.352
Croatia	18.8	23.8	-0.349	4.308	99.125
Czech Republic	48.5	19.5	0.102	4.507	-
Estonia	49.3	19.0	-0.03	5.152	99.863
Hungary	48.0	9.3	-0.233	4.712	99.374
Latvia	35.0	25.0	-1.034	4.935	99.896
Lithuania	42.6	24.1	-1.065	5.198	99.816
Montenegro	22.3	14.8	0.049	-	98.442
Poland	38.7	34.3	-0.013	5.171	99.748
Romania	43.2	13.5	-0.565	3.073	98.604
Slovakia	48.6	18.7	0.12	4.057	-
Slovenia	32.0	33.3	0.162	5.681	99.701
United States	43.8	18.3	0.716	5.42	-
China	64.6	23.4	0.494	1.907	95.124

Source: World Bank API.

Table 6.2 Country ranking by political risk

Country	Score
Slovenia	1.93
Estonia	1.96
Latvia	2.07
Poland	2.21
Czech Republic	2.21
Lithuania	2.36
Slovakia	2.64
Hungary	3.18
Bulgaria	3.29
Romania	3.46
Serbia	3.68
Croatia	3.68
Montenegro	3.89
Macedonia	4.07
Albania	4.14
Bosnia and Herzegovina	4.46
Kosovo	5.14

Note: The democracy scores and regime ratings are based on a scale of 1 to 7, with 1 representing the highest level of democratic progress and 7 the lowest. The 2015 ratings reflect the period January 1 through December 31, 2014.[1]

There is a renewed interest in how the political risk affects multinational corporations operating in emerging markets, and much of the research has focused on the relationship between democratic institutions and the flow of FDI. Nathan Jensen finds, for example, the democratic regimes

---

[1] *Nations in Transit* is the only comprehensive, comparative, and multidimensional study of reform in the former communist states of Europe and Eurasia. *Nations in Transit* tracks the reform record of 29 countries and administrative areas and provides Freedom House's most in-depth data about this vast and important region. The 2014 edition covers events from January 1 through December 31, 2013. It is an updated edition of surveys published in 2013, 2012, 2011, 2010, 2009, 2008, 2007, 2006, 2005, 2004, 2003, 2002, 2001, 1999–2000, 1998, 1997, and 1995. For information, see www.freedomhouse.org/report-types/nations-transit#.VdSJr86lSLg

reduce risks for multinational investors, specifically through increasing constraints on the executive.[2]

These relationships, and the variables noted in the Freedom House rankings, will be explored in more detail in country-specific case studies in this chapter. Finally, the chapter will conclude with a discussion on the merits and challenges of attempting to quantify and index political risk.

The next section of this chapter will provide broader analysis and context for the results assigned to each state, including an update on consequential political events from 2015.

Bosnia and Herzegovina

In 1995, the presidents of Bosnia, Croatia, and Serbia signed a General Framework Agreement for Peace to end the war in Bosnia. Also known as the "Dayton Accords," the treaty preserved Bosnia as a single state made up of two parts, the Bosniak-Croat Federation and the Bosnian Serb Republic, with Sarajevo remaining as the undivided capital city. The Bosnian administration split into two distinct entities: the Bosnia-Herzegovina Federation, composed of 10 cantons, and the Bosnian-Serb Republic. The complexity of this structure weakens the central executive power, led by the Prime Minister Vjekoslav Bevanda, a Bosnian Croat. The rotating presidency chaired between the three representatives of the Bosnian Muslim, Croatian Catholic, and Serbian orthodox communities maintains political inertia and struggles to transcend the ethnic divisions.[3]

In this context, widespread frustration has increased, culminating in February 2014, in an unprecedented outbreak of violence since peace was restored in 1995.[4] Exasperated by the negligent attitudes of privatized companies and unpaid wages for several months, workers initiated protests and demonstrations. Although most social classes and ethnic groups joined the protest, the movement was strongest within the Bosnia-Herzegovina Federation, where nearly half of the prime ministers resigned. This situation highlights the deep unease caused by widespread

---

[2] Jensen (2008).

[3] For more information on the impact of the Dayton Accords, see Gelazis (2005).

[4] Dzidic (2014).

corruption in a country that had demonstrated the struggle of undertaking reforms. Compounded by widespread flooding that directly affected around one-quarter of the country's population, the lack of coordination and a late response increased frustration against the ruling political class as a whole.[5]

The country held legislative and presidential elections in October 2014, which focused mainly on economic and social issues: allegedly corrupt politics, stagnation, and high unemployment. At the time of the elections, the unemployment rate in Bosnia was roughly 27.5 percent, consistently among the highest in the Balkans. Two in three young people reported being jobless. Meanwhile, the salary of lawmakers was six times the country's average wage, making Bosnia's members of parliament among the richest in Europe.[6]

Voter turnout, however, suggests that citizens did not view the elections as an opportunity to change the country's fortunes. The National Democratic Institute reported that more than 90 percent of citizens surveyed believed the country was moving in the wrong direction and 75 percent were dissatisfied with the performance of governing institutions. Those who did vote supported traditionally "national" parties— SDA (Bosnika); HDZ BiH (Croat); and SNSD (Serb). Thus, ethnic identity continued to be the main driver of politics.[7]

Meanwhile, in February 2014, the European Commission announced the end of negotiations regarding European Union (EU) membership, after 7 years of discussions, given the lack of reforms undertaken by the authorities. All levels of government are going to be faced with a dire economic situation. Following the census in spring 2015, the first since the Dayton Accords, political analysts expect to see ethnicity continue to frame political negotiations and the work of government. Finally, the business environment is hampered by corruption, inefficiency in the administrative and judicial systems, as well as the size of the informal sector.

Table 6.3 displays a series of ratings across various government indicators for Bosnia and Herzegovina.

---

[5] Thomas (2014); *The Guardian* (2014).

[6] Nardelli, Dzidic, and Jukic (2014).

[7] Lonely Planet (2014).

Table 6.3 Bosnia and Herzegovina—Nations in Transition Scores (2014)

	Nations in Transit Ratings and Averaged Scores									
	2005	2006	2007	2008	2009	2010	2011	2012	2013	2014
Electoral Process	3.25	3.00	3.00	3.00	3.00	3.25	3.25	3.25	3.25	3.25
Civil Society	3.75	3.75	3.50	3.50	3.50	3.50	3.50	3.50	3.50	3.50
Independent Media	4.00	4.00	4.00	4.25	4.50	4.50	4.75	4.75	4.75	4.75
National Democratic Governance	4.75	4.75	4.75	5.00	5.00	5.25	5.25	5.50	5.50	5.75
Local Democratic Governance	4.75	4.75	4.75	4.75	4.75	4.75	4.75	4.75	4.75	4.75
Judicial Framework and Independence	4.25	4.00	4.00	4.00	4.00	4.00	4.25	4.25	4.25	4.25
Corruption	4.50	4.25	4.25	4.25	4.50	4.50	4.50	4.50	4.75	4.75
Democracy Score	4.18	4.07	4.04	4.11	4.18	4.25	4.32	4.36	4.39	4.43

Note: The ratings are based on a scale of 1 to 7, with 1 representing the highest level of democratic progress and 7 the lowest. The democracy score is an average of ratings for the categories tracked in a given year.
Source: The data above are drawn from The World Bank, World Development Indicators 2014.

Bulgaria

As a post-communist state, Bulgaria has developed a system of democratic governance, joined North Atlantic Treaty Organization (NATO) in 2004 and the EU in 2007. The government has held a number of free and fair general, presidential, and local elections.

Over the last few years, however, the country has showed signs of increasing political instability in key democratic institutions. Since 2012, Bulgaria has had three governments, and inefficiency and graft within the political system, including the judiciary, are considered major obstacles to fighting high-level corruption and organized crime.[8] In 2014, an alleged personal conflict between Deylan Peevski, media mogul and politician, and Tsvetan Vassilev, the owner of Corporate Commercial Bank (KTB), led to a banking crisis, a government bailout, and numerous arrests.[9]

Further, the most recent parliament, elected in October 2014, became the most fragmented in Bulgaria's democratic history. With eight parties and alliances winning seats, the number of parties doubled compared to the previous parliament.[10] The Citizens for European Development of Bulgaria (GERB) emerged as the strongest party, returning to power after being ousted in February 2013. The next challenge to Bulgaria's political system, as depicted in Table 6.4, came in 2015, when the coalition government worked to preserve its majority in the parliament and simultaneously implement unpopular reforms.

Croatia

Croatia has been unable to gain momentum in implementing reforms as part of membership in the EU. Economic indicators show that the economy contracted for 12 successive quarters as the Social Democratic Party of Croatia (SDP) and its opposition, Croatian Democratic Union (HDZ), continued their political battles over the legacy of Yugoslav

---

[8] G.K. (2014); Novinite.com (2015); R.P. (2015).

[9] Brunwasser (2013); V.V.B. (2013); "Bulgarian Protests: Students Determined to Overthrow System" (2013).

[10] "Bulgaria's 2014 parliamentary election: CEC announces final results" (2014).

Table 6.4 Bulgaria—Nations in Transition Scores (2015)

	Nations in Transit Ratings and Averaged Scores									
	2006	2007	2008	2009	2010	2011	2012	2013	2014	2015
Electoral Process	1.75	1.75	1.75	1.75	1.75	1.75	2.00	2.00	2.25	2.25
Civil Society	2.75	2.50	2.50	2.50	2.50	2.50	2.50	2.50	2.25	2.25
Independent Media	3.25	3.50	3.50	3.75	3.75	3.75	3.75	4.00	4.00	4.00
National Democratic Governance	3.00	3.00	3.00	3.25	3.25	3.50	3.50	3.50	3.75	3.75
Local Democratic Governance	3.00	3.00	3.00	3.00	3.00	3.00	3.00	3.00	3.00	3.00
Judicial Framework and Independence	3.00	2.75	2.75	3.00	3.00	3.00	3.25	3.25	3.25	3.50
Corruption	3.75	3.75	3.50	4.00	4.00	4.00	4.00	4.00	4.25	4.25
Democracy Score	2.93	2.89	2.86	3.04	3.04	3.07	3.14	3.18	3.25	3.29

Note: The ratings are based on a scale of 1 to 7, with 1 representing the highest level of democratic progress and 7 the lowest. The democracy score is an average of ratings for the categories tracked in a given year.
Source: The data above are drawn from The World Bank, World Development Indicators 2015.

communism and privatization efforts in the 1990s. The inability to provide effective political and economic leadership has led decreasing citizen confidence in government and the emergence of a third party, Croatian Sustainable Development (ORaH).

In the context of an open, transparent society, the relationship between business interests and government officials is unhealthy. In November 2012, former Prime Minister Ivo Sanader was convicted on charges of bribery and kickbacks involving nearly 13 million euros in the biggest corruption trial in Croatia's history. In a prebankruptcy settlement, the government also forgave taxes owed by media conglomerate Europapress Holding (EPH), leading to criticisms of lack of transparency and favorable treatment in return for positive media coverage. There is widespread concern that other interests groups are using the referendum process to circumvent the legislature, some attempting to address economic concerns and others targeted at restricting the rights of minorities.

Even with the high-profile arrest of Zagreb mayor Milan Bandic in October 2014 on suspicion of corruption and abuse of office, public distrust in government still remains high. Thus, Croatia's governing parties are preparing for confrontational campaigns in 2015. Table 6.5 provides the country's scores.

Czech Republic

The Czech Republic has established stable, democratic institutions and a vibrant civil society. In 2013, the country experienced a handful of national politics scandals, most notably the spying scandal and resignation of former Prime Minister Petr Nečas.[11] Centering on his alleged love affair with his chief of staff, the abuse of secret services, and alleged corruption, the center-right prime minister and his cabinet were forced out of office nearly a year before elections were scheduled (Table 6.6).

While the new government formed under Prime Minister Bohuslav Sobotka places significant emphasis on fighting corruption, most analysts view the passage of the Law on Civil Service and other reforms as

---

[11] K.S. (2013).

Table 6.5 *Croatia—Nations in Transition Scores (2015)*

		Nations in Transit Ratings and Averaged Scores								
	2006	2007	2008	2009	2010	2011	2012	2013	2014	2015
Electoral Process	3.25	3.25	3.25	3.25	3.25	3.25	3.25	3.25	3.25	3.25
Civil Society	2.75	2.75	2.75	2.75	2.75	2.50	2.50	2.50	2.75	2.75
Independent Media	3.75	4.00	3.75	4.00	4.00	4.00	4.00	4.00	4.00	4.00
National Democratic Governance	3.50	3.50	3.25	3.50	3.50	3.50	3.50	3.50	3.50	3.50
Local Democratic Governance	3.75	3.75	3.75	3.75	3.75	3.75	3.75	3.75	3.75	3.75
Judicial Framework and Independence	4.25	4.25	4.25	4.25	4.25	4.25	4.25	4.25	4.50	4.50
Corruption	4.75	4.75	4.50	4.50	4.50	4.25	4.00	4.00	4.00	4.00
Democracy Score	3.71	3.75	3.64	3.71	3.71	3.64	3.61	3.61	3.68	3.68

Note: The ratings are based on a scale of 1 to 7, with 1 representing the highest level of democratic progress and 7 the lowest. The democracy score is an average of ratings for the categories tracked in a given year.
Source: The data above are drawn from The World Bank, World Development Indicators 2015.

Table 6.6 Czech Republic—Nations in Transition Scores (2015)

| | Nations in Transit Ratings and Averaged Scores | | | | | | | | | |
	2006	2007	2008	2009	2010	2011	2012	2013	2014	2015
Electoral Process	2.00	1.75	1.75	1.50	1.50	1.25	1.25	1.25	1.25	1.25
Civil Society	1.50	1.50	1.25	1.50	1.75	1.75	1.75	1.75	1.75	1.75
Independent Media	2.00	2.25	2.25	2.25	2.50	2.50	2.50	2.50	2.75	2.75
National Democratic Governance	2.50	3.00	2.75	2.75	2.75	2.75	2.75	2.75	3.00	2.75
Local Democratic Governance	2.00	1.75	1.75	1.75	1.75	1.75	1.75	1.75	1.75	1.75
Judicial Framework and Independence	2.25	2.00	2.00	2.25	2.00	2.00	2.00	1.75	1.75	1.75
Corruption	3.50	3.50	3.25	3.25	3.25	3.25	3.25	3.25	3.50	3.50
Democracy Score	2.25	2.25	2.14	2.18	2.21	2.18	2.18	2.14	2.25	2.21

Note: The ratings are based on a scale of 1 to 7, with 1 representing the highest level of democratic progress and 7 the lowest. The democracy score is an average of ratings for the categories tracked in a given year.

Source: The data above are drawn from The World Bank, World Development Indicators 2015.

modest.[12] The government maintained high approval ratings throughout the year, with around 40 to 50 percent of respondents expressing trust in the coalition.[13]

Former Prime Minister Milos Zeman won the first direct Czech presidential election in January 2013, beating conservative Foreign Minister Karel Schwarzenberg by a margin of 55 to 45 percent. Unlike his predecessor, the notoriously euro-sceptic Vaclav Klaus, President Zeman describes himself as a euro-federalist and has advocated closer European integration, though he believes that the Czech Republic should take its time over joining the euro.[14] Other statements from the president defending authoritarian regimes around the world, including China, questioning Western involvement in Ukraine, and xenophobic anti-Islamic speeches have drawn severe criticism from the population. By the end of 2014, the president's approval ratings had significantly dropped.[15]

The government has been eager to support exports, including signing a joint declaration with China in April 2014. Economic cooperation will also be supported by new direct flight connections, operational in October 2015, from Prague to Beijing with Hainan Airlines (and planned route from Prague to Shanghai). These projects are strongly supported by the Czech government, in addition to a plan to create economic and technological zones for Chinese investors in the Moravia-Silesia Region. The agreement did draw criticism from the Czech public because of a clause noting Tibet is Chinese territory, but the biggest challenge facing the government in this new bilateral trade relationship is the Czech deficit in the bilateral trade. The imports from China to the Czech Republic reached 359 billion Kč and Czech exports to China 42 billion Kč in 2014, creating a deficit of 317 billion Kč.[16]

The coalition government will need to continue to work together to maintain stability and achieve successful legislative reform, and with no elections scheduled for 2015 there is reason to be optimistic. The

---

[12] Mráz (2015).
[13] Kunštát (2015).
[14] Czech Republic Profile—Leaders (2015).
[15] Czech Republic Profile—Leaders (2015).
[16] Du Bois and Davidova (2015).

government should also benefit from continuing improvement in the economy, without much danger of slipping back into recession.

Estonia

In early 2014, the Estonian government formed a new cabinet following the resignation of 9-year veteran Prime Minister Andrus Ansip, who accepted a new position working with the European Commission. The country held elections in 2015 and re-elected the governing Reform Party, led by Prime Minister Taavi Roivas. The youngest Prime Minister in Europe, Roivas called for an "Estonian-minded government" in the weeks leading up to the election.

Perhaps reflecting the most significant issue facing Estonia today is public political debate by economic issues and fears over defense due to Russia's actions in Ukraine. Estonia has seen a number of airspace violations by Russia, and last year a security official was detained by Russia and accused of spying. Prime Minister Roivas voiced concerns that Russia could seek to destabilize other former Soviet states following the conflict in Ukraine, while the Centre Party leader, Edgar Saavisar, favors a friendlier approach to Moscow, and has previously suggested that Russia's annexation of Crimea could be legitimate. Saavisar's position reflects nearly one quarter of Estonia's 1.3 million populations who self-identify as ethnic Russians, and many of who are Centre Party supporters.[17] Savisar lost some political momentum for his case, however, when he was arrested on charges of bribery in September 2015.

Estonia is consistently acknowledged as one of the least corrupt countries in the EU, according to most recent 2014 and 2015 indexes. Key anticorruption measures adopted in 2013 established a framework for enhancing accountability in the civil sector. Although some scandals involving bribery and political influence led to public discussions about lobbying practices, the country remains very highly rated in terms of transparency (Table 6.7).[18]

---

[17] Mardiste (2015).
[18] Hinsburg, Matt, and Vinni (2015).

Table 6.7 Estonia—Nations in Transition Scores (2015)

		Nations in Transit Ratings and Averaged Scores									
	2006	2007	2008	2009	2010	2011	2012	2013	2014	2015
Electoral Process	1.50	1.50	1.50	1.50	1.75	1.75	1.75	1.75	1.75	1.75
Civil Society	2.00	2.00	1.75	1.75	1.75	1.75	1.75	1.75	1.75	1.75
Independent Media	1.50	1.50	1.50	1.50	1.50	1.50	1.50	1.50	1.50	1.50
National Democratic Governance	2.25	2.25	2.25	2.25	2.25	2.25	2.25	2.25	2.25	2.25
Local Democratic Governance	2.50	2.50	2.50	2.50	2.50	2.50	2.50	2.50	2.50	2.50
Judicial Framework and Independence	1.50	1.50	1.50	1.50	1.50	1.50	1.50	1.50	1.50	1.50
Corruption	2.50	2.50	2.50	2.50	2.50	2.25	2.25	2.50	2.50	2.50
Democracy Score	1.96	1.96	1.93	1.93	1.96	1.93	1.93	1.96	1.96	1.96

Note: The ratings are based on a scale of 1 to 7, with 1 representing the highest level of democratic progress and 7 the lowest. The democracy score is an average of ratings for the categories tracked in a given year.

Source: The data above are drawn from The World Bank, World Development Indicators 2015.

Hungry

The government of Prime Minister Viktor Orbán consists of the right-wing Young Democrats' Alliance-Hungary Civic Union (Fidesz) and the Christian Democratic People's Party (KDNP). It was elected for a second 4-year term in 2014, winning a two-third majority control of the parliament. Those assessing democratic governance, transparency, and judicial independence in Hungary have good reasons to be concerned. In a July 2014 speech, Orbán openly discussed his plans to construct an "illiberal democracy."

The Fidesz-controlled legislature passed a law in 2010 that established a body, appointed by the parliament—and thus by Fidesz—to regulate the media. The law made it a crime, punishable by fines of up to 900,000 dollars, to publish "imbalanced news coverage" or material deemed "insulting" to a group or "the majority" or that insulted "public morality."

In 2011, parliament passed a law on the "Right of Freedom of Conscience and Religion," which bore the same relation to freedom of conscience that the media law did to freedom of speech. The law required religious organizations to gain official approval through a two-third vote of parliament, thus creating separate classes of favored and nonfavored faiths.

Peter Kreko, Director of the Political Capital Institute, a think tank in Budapest, admits that he is alarmed by the racial rhetoric Orbán has employed since the refugee crisis began because he is worried that it works. "At bottom," he says, "the real source of Orbán's power is the popularity of his ideas." In that sense, the problem lies with the Hungarian people. As James Staub and other political analysts note, not long ago Hungary was widely considered the most progressive of the ex-Soviet states. Growing disillusionment with democracy and the free market over the last decade might make Hungarians receptive to ideas they once would have rejected.

These circumstances are further complicated by close ties between political and economic elites, which remain a major source of corruption for the state. Despite several corruption scandals surfacing in Hungarian media, whistleblowers and the U.S. State Department allege

Table 6.8 Hungary—Nations in Transit Scores (2015)

	Nations in Transit Ratings and Averaged Scores									
	2006	2007	2008	2009	2010	2011	2012	2013	2014	2015
Electoral Process	1.25	1.75	1.75	1.75	1.75	1.75	2.25	2.25	2.25	2.75
Civil Society	1.25	1.50	1.50	1.75	1.75	2.00	2.00	2.25	2.25	2.50
Independent Media	2.50	2.50	2.50	2.50	2.75	3.25	3.50	3.50	3.50	3.75
National Democratic Governance	2.00	2.25	2.25	2.50	2.50	3.00	3.50	3.50	3.75	3.75
Local Democratic Governance	2.25	2.25	2.25	2.50	2.50	2.50	2.50	2.75	2.75	3.00
Judicial Framework and Independence	1.75	1.75	1.75	1.75	2.00	2.25	2.75	2.50	2.50	2.75
Corruption	3.00	3.00	3.00	3.25	3.50	3.50	3.50	3.50	3.75	3.75
Democracy Score	2.00	2.14	2.14	2.29	2.39	2.61	2.86	2.89	2.96	3.18

Note: The ratings are based on a scale of 1 to 7, with 1 representing the highest level of democratic progress and 7 the lowest. The democracy score is an average of ratings for the categories tracked in a given year.
Source: The data above are drawn from The World Bank, World Development Indicators 2015.

that numerous cases have gone uninvestigated by the government.[19] Hungary's corruption rating remains unchanged for the current year, despite ratings declining in nearly every other category for the Nations in Transit scores (Table 6.8).

Latvia

In January 2014, Laimdota Straujuma, an economist and member of the center-right Unity Party, was sworn in as Latvia's first female prime minister. She resigned in December 2015, however, amid political infighting within her party's ruling coalition, leaving the small Baltic nation without a strong government at a time of growing tension with neighboring Russia.[20]

Despite these setbacks in national democratic governance, Latvia continues to craft a new national vision for the state. It successfully administered European Parliament and Saeima elections in 2014 and assumed the presidency of the Council of the EU in 2015.

The security crisis in Eastern Ukraine remains a significant concern for Latvian domestic and foreign policy, as in Estonia and other border states. Russian warships and military planes operated very closely to Latvian waters and airspace throughout 2014, prompting widespread fears that Latvia's Russian minority might be the next to be "liberated" by Moscow.[21] According to Freedom House and other reports, the Latvian government leadership "maintained a united position on the need to protect Latvia from potential Russian military aggression and lobbied hard to increase the presence of NATO troops in Latvia."[22]

Public opinion polls from March 2014 indicate that an increased NATO presence was supported by 50 percent of respondents.[23] By year's

---

[19] Human Rights First (2014).

[20] "Apstiprināta jaunā valdība Laimdotas Straujumas vadībā" (2014); Kaza (2015).

[21] "Šogad Krievijas bruņoto spēku lidmašīnas un kuģi Latvijai pietuvojušies vairāk nekā 250 reizes" (2014).

[22] Bukovskis and Sprūds (2015).

[23] Apriņķis.lv (2014).

Table 6.9 Latvia—Nations in Transition Scores (2015)

			Nations in Transit Ratings and Averaged Scores							
	2006	2007	2008	2009	2010	2011	2012	2013	2014	2015
Electoral Process	1.75	2.00	2.00	2.00	2.00	1.75	1.75	1.75	1.75	1.75
Civil Society	1.75	1.75	1.75	1.75	1.75	1.75	1.75	1.75	1.75	1.75
Independent Media	1.50	1.50	1.75	1.75	1.75	1.75	1.75	1.75	2.00	2.00
National Democratic Governance	2.00	2.00	2.00	2.50	2.50	2.25	2.25	2.25	2.00	2.00
Local Democratic Governance	2.50	2.50	2.25	2.25	2.25	2.25	2.25	2.25	2.25	2.25
Judicial Framework and Independence	1.75	1.75	1.75	1.75	1.75	1.75	1.75	1.75	1.75	1.75
Corruption	3.25	3.00	3.00	3.25	3.25	3.50	3.25	3.00	3.00	3.00
Democracy Score	2.07	2.07	2.07	2.18	2.18	2.14	2.11	2.07	2.07	2.07

Note: The ratings are based on a scale of 1 to 7, with 1 representing the highest level of democratic progress and 7 the lowest. The democracy score is an average of ratings for the categories tracked in a given year.

Source: The data above are drawn from The World Bank, World Development Indicators 2015.

end, Latvia—together with its Baltic neighbors, Estonia and Lithuania—had received commitments of military solidarity from NATO as a whole and several individual member states, including the United Kingdom, the United States, Germany, and Norway. Latvia also pledged to increase military spending to 2 percent of gross domestic product (GDP) by the year 2020, with special emphasis on improved weaponry and airspace defense (Table 6.9).[24]

Lithuania

In May 2014, incumbent President Dalia Grybauskaitė won the presidential run-off against Zigmantas Balčytis, a member of the LSDP (Social Democratic Party of Lithuania). Popular among Lithuanians, Grybauskaitė became the first Lithuanian president elected to two consecutive terms. Lithuanian politics are composed of shifting coalitions among several different parties. The two largest minority groups, Polish (6.6 percent of the population) and Russian (5.8 percent), are represented by the LLRA (Electoral Action of Poles in Lithuania) and the Russian Alliance parties who plan to form a coalition for local elections in 2015.

While corruption remains an issue in Lithuania, Freedom House and other sources note that progress has been achieved. Lithuania ranked 39 out of 175 countries and territories in Transparency International's 2014 Corruption Perceptions Index.[25] The EU has noted Lithuania's strong commitment to fighting corruption and venerable anticorruption legal framework. However, the EU also noted room for improvement; Lithuania has the highest percentage in the EU of people who have been asked or were expected to pay a bribe: 29 percent.

In 2014, Grybauskaitė declared that she would not approve ministers whose deputies were included on a so-called "blacklist" created by the Secret Investigation Service (STT). The blacklist contained eight vice-ministers who were allegedly involved in corruption cases. All eight vice-ministers rapidly resigned, including one from the ministry of justice,

---

[24] Lsm.lv (2014).
[25] Transparency International (2014).

one from the ministry of agriculture, three from the ministry of environment, and three from the ministry of transport and communications.

After completing its 6-month presidency at the Council of the EU, Lithuania prepared for the introduction of the euro despite public ambivalence.[26] In January of 2015, the council recognized Lithuania's accession to the eurozone and the country became its 19th member. Lithuania actively pushed for membership in the Organization for Economic Cooperation and Development (OECD), and in October 2015 the OECD outlined a plan for Lithuanian accession. The Heritage Foundation increased its economic freedom score for Lithuania in 2015, raising the country to the 15th freest in the world.[27] Lithuania also improved on the World Economic Forum's Global Competitiveness Report in 2015, moving up to 5 spots to 36th place. This is the second year in a row that Lithuania has seen a significant rankings increase in both sets of reports (Table 6.10).

Poland

Although recent articles have praised CEE as a "tranquil port in emerging market storm," there are still reasons to be cautious.[28] In Poland, Central Europe's biggest economy and "anchor" of stability, will hold parliamentary elections in October that may bring a change of government. In Poland, CEE's biggest economy, the prime minister has the most powers, but the president wields clout as head of the armed forces, has a say in foreign policy and the power to veto legislation.

In this context, *Reuters* reports that the presidential election has become a dress rehearsal for the parliamentary vote, when Prime Minister Ewa Kopacz's center-right Civic Platform Party will face a strong challenge from the euro-sceptic Law and Justice Party (PiS), a significant frontrunner in the polls.[29]

---

[26] "Vyriausybės naujienlaiškis" (2014).
[27] Index of Economic Freedom (2015).
[28] Jones (2015).
[29] Goclowski and Florkiewicz (2015).

Table 6.10 Lithuania—Nations in Transition Scores (2015)

	2006	2007	2008	2009	2010	2011	2012	2013	2014	2015
Nations in Transit Ratings and Averaged Scores										
Electoral Process	1.75	1.75	1.75	1.75	1.75	1.75	1.75	2.00	2.00	2.00
Civil Society	1.50	1.75	1.75	1.75	1.75	1.75	1.75	1.75	1.75	1.75
Independent Media	1.75	1.75	1.75	1.75	1.75	1.75	2.00	2.00	2.25	2.25
National Democratic Governance	2.50	2.50	2.50	2.75	2.75	2.75	2.75	2.75	2.75	2.75
Local Democratic Governance	2.50	2.50	2.50	2.50	2.50	2.50	2.50	2.50	2.50	2.50
Judicial Framework and Independence	1.50	1.75	1.75	1.75	1.75	1.75	1.75	1.75	1.75	1.75
Corruption	4.00	4.00	3.75	3.75	3.50	3.50	3.50	3.50	3.50	3.50
Democracy Score	2.21	2.29	2.25	2.29	2.25	2.25	2.29	2.32	2.36	2.36

Note: The ratings are based on a scale of 1 to 7, with 1 representing the highest level of democratic progress and 7 the lowest. The democracy score is an average of ratings for the categories tracked in a given year.
Source: The data above are drawn from The World Bank, World Development Indicators 2015.

Although the government has a strong record on the economy and Poland was the only EU country to avoid recession after the 2008 financial crash (see Chapter 6), it is still struggling to counter a sense among voters that they want to see some fresh faces in power. The government also lost its strongest political asset last year when Donald Tusk left his position as prime minister to take a senior EU post in Brussels. In an interview in 2014, Rafal Pankowski, an expert on Poland's political Rights, expressed concerns about the impact of Tusks's departure: "Without him it is difficult to imagine how the party will survive and maintain the same level of support," he commented. "There is no successor who has the same track record as he does. He holds the party together."[30]

In May 2015, Polish President Bronsilaw Komorowski campaigned on a platform that he is a "safe pair of hands" on national security. That message appealed to voters following news about Russia's intervention in Ukraine, Poland could become the next target. Andrzej Duda, the conservative challenger, campaigned on a promise to lower the retirement age and warned that if Poland adopts the euro currency, which Komorowski has said he wants eventually to happen, the prices of goods will go up. On May 24, 2015, global media outlets reported that Komorowski conceded defeat to conservative challenger Duda, a result that set off alarms across the government. The victory for 43-year-old Duda marked the first major electoral win in almost a decade for his party, the opposition Law and Justice Party. It is close to the Catholic Church, socially conservative, and markets see it as less business-friendly than the governing Civic Platform. The situation was not helped when Poland's zloty currency fell 1 percent against the euro after the election exit poll was released (Table 6.11).

Romania

Many political analysts were surprised by the 2014 election of Klaus Iohannis, former Mayor of Sibiu and an ethnic German, as the next President of Romania. He achieved a record number of votes from nearly 400,000 Romanians living abroad, and with nearly 1.5 million Facebook followers he has more digital "fans" than most European politicians. His

---

[30] Day and Waterfeld (2014).

Table 6.11 Poland—Nations in Transition Scores (2015)

	2006	2007	2008	2009	2010	2011	2012	2013	2014	2015
	Nations in Transit Ratings and Averaged Scores									
Electoral Process	1.75	2.00	2.00	2.00	1.75	1.50	1.25	1.25	1.25	1.50
Civil Society	1.25	1.50	1.25	1.50	1.50	1.50	1.50	1.50	1.50	1.50
Independent Media	1.75	2.25	2.25	2.00	2.25	2.25	2.25	2.50	2.50	2.50
National Democratic Governance	2.75	3.25	3.50	3.25	3.25	2.75	2.50	2.50	2.50	2.50
Local Democratic Governance	2.00	2.25	2.25	2.00	1.75	1.75	1.75	1.75	1.50	1.50
Judicial Framework and Independence	2.25	2.25	2.50	2.25	2.50	2.50	2.50	2.50	2.50	2.50
Corruption	3.25	3.00	3.00	2.75	3.25	3.25	3.25	3.25	3.50	3.50
Democracy Score	2.14	2.36	2.39	2.25	2.32	2.21	2.14	2.18	2.18	2.21

Note: The ratings are based on a scale of 1 to 7, with 1 representing the highest level of democratic progress and 7 the lowest. The democracy score is an average of ratings for the categories tracked in a given year.

Source: The data above are drawn from The World Bank, World Development Indicators 2015.

victory over the political machine of Victor Ponta, the Prime Minister, is regarded as a strong commitment among Romanians for cleaner, more transparent politics.

In a recent survey, over 90 percent of Romanians expressed beliefs that graft is endemic among their political and economic elites. Freedom House and other corruption indexes noted that 2014 was the most successful year so far for the National Anticorruption Directorate (DNA). Prosecutors working with the organization secured important convictions in both the public and private sector, including exposing a serious corruption scandal that operated under four successive government administrations. All told, DNA prosecutors won more than 1,000 convictions and indicted more than 1,100 suspects in 2014; more than 90 percent of those indicted were convicted (Table 6.12).

Additionally, President Iohannis faces the difficult balance in foreign policy between positive relations with Russia and the EU. In the fall of 2015, he affirmed Romania's commitment to EU sanctions imposed on Russia for its actions in Ukraine and welcomed NATO's increasing presence in an increasingly insecure border region.[31]

Serbia

On the promise of economic revitalization and a commitment to anti-corruption, the Serbian Progressive Party (SNS) won nearly two-thirds of the seats in parliament in the 2014 elections. This mandate allowed the party to adopt new legislation enabling future EU membership and efforts to normalize relations with Kosovo, which marks a sharp departure from the ultra-nationalism espoused by the state for decades following the break-up of Yugoslavia.[32]

The government, under the leadership of Prime Minister Aleksandar Vucic, is attempting to attract foreign investors and improve the environment for doing business in Serbia. Traditionally a strong ally of the

---

[31] "Romania Supports Sanctions Against Russia until Full Implementation of Minsk Agreements" (2015).

[32] "Serbian Prime Minister Vucic Pledges Millions to Srebrenica" (2015).

Table 6.12 Romania—Nations in Transition Scores (2015)

		Nations in Transit Ratings and Averaged Scores								
	2006	2007	2008	2009	2010	2011	2012	2013	2014	2015
Electoral Process	2.75	2.75	2.75	2.50	2.75	2.75	3.00	3.00	3.00	3.25
Civil Society	2.25	2.25	2.25	2.50	2.50	2.50	2.50	2.50	2.50	2.50
Independent Media	4.00	3.75	3.75	3.75	4.00	4.00	4.00	4.25	4.25	4.25
National Democratic Governance	3.50	3.50	3.75	3.75	4.00	3.75	3.75	4.00	3.75	3.75
Local Democratic Governance	3.00	3.00	3.00	3.00	3.00	3.00	3.00	3.00	3.00	3.00
Judicial Framework and Independence	4.00	3.75	4.00	4.00	4.00	4.00	3.75	3.75	3.75	3.75
Corruption	4.25	4.00	4.00	4.00	4.00	4.00	4.00	4.00	4.00	3.75
Democracy Score	3.39	3.29	3.36	3.36	3.46	3.43	3.43	3.50	3.46	3.46

Note: The ratings are based on a scale of 1 to 7, with 1 representing the highest level of democratic progress and 7 the lowest. The democracy score is an average of ratings for the categories tracked in a given year.
Source: The data above are drawn from The World Bank, World Development Indicators 2015.

Table 6.13 *Serbia—Nations in Transition Scores (2015)*

Nations in Transit Ratings and Averaged Scores										
	2006	2007	2008	2009	2010	2011	2012	2013	2014	2015
Electoral Process	3.25	3.25	3.25	3.25	3.25	3.25	3.25	3.25	3.25	3.25
Civil Society	2.75	2.75	2.75	2.75	2.50	2.25	2.25	2.25	2.25	2.25
Independent Media	3.25	3.50	3.75	3.75	4.00	4.00	4.00	4.00	4.00	4.25
National Democratic Governance	4.00	3.75	4.00	4.00	3.75	3.75	3.75	3.75	3.75	3.75
Local Democratic Governance	3.75	3.75	3.75	3.75	3.50	3.50	3.50	3.50	3.50	3.50
Judicial Framework and Independence	4.25	4.25	4.50	4.50	4.50	4.50	4.50	4.50	4.50	4.50
Corruption	4.75	4.50	4.50	4.50	4.50	4.25	4.25	4.25	4.25	4.25
Democracy Score	3.71	3.68	3.79	3.79	3.71	3.64	3.64	3.64	3.64	3.68

Note: The ratings are based on a scale of 1 to 7, with 1 representing the highest level of democratic progress and 7 the lowest. The democracy score is an average of ratings for the categories tracked in a given year.
Source: The data above are drawn from The World Bank, World Development Indicators 2015.

Russian government, Vucic has signaled a strong desire to align Serbia with the United States and EU.[33] Jose Manuel Barroso, then European Commission President, hailed accession negotiations as "an entirely new chapter in our relations and a major success."[34] EU officials, however, recently emphasized that no new members would be taken before 2020. For Serbia, the key will be the implementation of the 2013 Kosovo agreement, improvement in the efficiency of its judicial processes, and the SNS Party's ability to make good on its anticorruption promises (Table 6.13).

Slovakia

The 2014 elections marked a historic shift in Slovak electoral politics. In a surprise upset, Robert Fico, Slovakia's Prime Minister, lost the presidential run-off election to Andrej Kiska, a businessman and philanthropist. Prior to the March election, Fico dominated domestic politics in Slovakia for most of the last decade.[35] This was followed by the equally surprising resignation of Pavol Paška, then fellow Smer Party Speaker of Parliament, following a corruption scandal.[36]

These political shifts highlight the unfortunate lack of transparency, as well as continuing clientelist and corrupt practices that persist across the country. No prosecutions moved forward against prominent officials, including Paška in 2014.

Slovakia does have a progressive institutional framework for fighting graft and improving transparency in the public sphere but corruption remains a serious problem, most notably in public procurement and the health sector.[37] The Slovak constitution does include a provision on conflict of interest, barring the president, cabinet members, constitutional court justices, and other top officials from pursuing any business

---

[33] Skrpec (2015).
[34] European Commission (2014).
[35] Pleso (2014).
[36] Cuprik (2014).
[37] Cunningham (2015).

activities, receiving pay for brokering deals between the government and private entities or corporations, or receiving income in excess of the minimum wage generated by a side job.[38] However, public officials are not required to give a full public accounting of the sources of their income and there are no laws regulating the private gifts they accept.[39]

According to Transparency International's 2014 Corruption Perceptions Index, one in five households in Slovakia reported paying a bribe for health care every year, and health care was perceived as the sector most affected by corruption. Slovakia's ranking in the Transparency International study improved in 2014, primarily because of the new law protecting whistleblowers, new legislation for the formation of political parties, and the proposed e-marketplace for public procurement bids (although the report expressed reservations about implementation of new laws) (Table 6.14).[40]

As in many of the other CEE states, President Kiska also faces the diplomatic and foreign policy challenges of balancing relations with Russia and the West. In a statement to the NATO2020 conference, he remarked,

This new situation is not a challenge only for military strategic planners. It is a profound political and psychological challenge. Because the single most important and historically verified purpose of NATO is not only its capacity to defend sovereignty of members states by military force. But it's also our ability to deter anyone who would like to think about testing their own capacity.[41]

In a follow-up tweet to the conference, he reinforced his belief that "NATO is not a winter coat" to be put on when cold, but that the alliance requires a more enduring commitment from all parties to be an effective deterrent.

---

[38] Dumbrovsky (2015).
[39] Terenzani-Stankova (2014).
[40] Transparency International (2014); Radka Minecherová (2014).
[41] Andrej Kiska (2015).

Table 6.14 Slovakia—Nations in Transition Scores (2015)

	Nations in Transit Ratings and Averaged Scores									
	2006	2007	2008	2009	2010	2011	2012	2013	2014	2015
Electoral Process	1.25	1.50	1.50	1.50	1.75	1.50	1.50	1.50	1.50	1.50
Civil Society	1.25	1.50	1.50	1.75	1.75	1.75	1.75	1.75	1.75	1.75
Independent Media	2.25	2.25	2.50	2.75	3.00	3.00	2.75	2.75	2.75	3.00
National Democratic Governance	2.00	2.25	2.50	2.75	3.00	2.75	2.75	2.75	3.00	3.00
Local Democratic Governance	2.00	2.00	2.25	2.50	2.50	2.50	2.50	2.50	2.50	2.50
Judicial Framework and Independence	2.00	2.25	2.50	2.75	3.00	2.75	2.75	3.00	3.00	3.00
Corruption	3.00	3.25	3.25	3.25	3.75	3.50	3.50	3.75	3.75	3.75
Democracy Score	1.96	2.14	2.29	2.46	2.68	2.54	2.50	2.57	2.61	2.64

Note: The ratings are based on a scale of 1 to 7, with 1 representing the highest level of democratic progress and 7 the lowest. The democracy score is an average of ratings for the categories tracked in a given year.
Source: The data above are drawn from The World Bank, World Development Indicators 2015.

Slovenia

Slovenia is one of the most politically and economically integrated countries in the region, joining the United Nations in 1992, the Council of Europe in 1993, and the EU and NATO in 2004. The state adopted the euro currency and entered the Schengen Area in 2007, followed by achieving full membership in the OECD in 2010.

As Slovenia's economy showed strong signs of recovery in 2014, political conflict and instability set in. Prime Minister Alenka Bratusek resigned from her post after serving only 13 months, leaving no clear leadership or mandate for the government. This prompted concerns among political analysts who viewed the instability as a risk to the structural reform agenda from 2014 to 2015, including the privatization of key state-owned enterprises.[42] Since that time, Bratusek has been under investigation by Slovenian antigraft authorities on suspicion of abuse of power.[43]

In August 2014, Dr. Miro Cerar assumed the position of prime minister and emphasized long-term sustainable economic growth as the first priority of his administration. In an initial step, the state adopted the asset management strategy for state-owned enterprises, and this commitment was echoed in his statements at the FDI Summit of 2014. When interviewed by the *Slovenia Times*, Cerar reiterated that the government has been "preparing and implementing measures to lower the administrative burden, amend labor legislation and lower labor costs. On the other hand, we are creating better business conditions by building and maintaining the infrastructure, promoting and further developing our educational system and innovation-oriented ecosystems."[44] Cerar may be able to achieve many of these goals, given the consistent and stable support he receives from the National Assembly.

An ongoing issue that may distract from Cerar's economic reforms is an open border dispute with Croatia. In 2009, the two former Yugoslav states agreed to a deal wherein the five-member tribunal would reach a binding decision on 5 square miles (13 km^2) of mostly uninhabited

---

[42] "Slovenia Prime Minister Alenka Bratusek Resigns" (2014).

[43] "Police Search Home of Former Slovenian Premier" (2015).

[44] Drolc (2015).

land and coastline. Both Slovenia and Croatia were asked to propose one member for the panel and a key element of impartiality was that no member discusses the tribunal's work with their government. Slovenia has only 29 miles (46 km) of coastline and argues that its access to international waters hangs in the balance as Croatia, with its 1,050 miles of coastline seeks to draw the border right through the middle of the disputed bay.[45] Croatia recently withdrew from negotiations, calling them "dead" and accusing Slovenia of compromising the integrity of the panel, and Slovenia continues to have issues finding a satisfactory appointment to represent their interests at arbitration. The panel was scheduled to set an agreement by the end of 2015, but no information has been released to date (Table 6.15).

Assessing Political Risk

As barriers to regional and international trade are lowered, investors continue to seek new opportunities in emerging markets around the world. As we have seen in the individual case studies, these markets are vulnerable to a wide range of forces, known as political risk, which are beyond the control of potential investors. These risks might include corruption, unstable government institutions, reforming financial systems, uncertain legal systems or regulatory regimes, and even currency instability.

Techniques for assessing these risks are wide ranging, from traditional methods employing comparative ratings and mapping systems (as illustrated in the case studies of this chapter), to special reports, expert systems, modeling, and logit analysis. No assessment method is perfect, and correlating the individual variables does not often yield accurate measurements of potential loss generated by political risk.

Yet, companies acknowledge that no matter their size, they must consider the political environment when planning to conduct business abroad. As noted in previous publications within this series, "one of the most undeniable and crucial realities of international business is that both host and home government are integral partners."[46]

---

[45] "Croatia to Pull Out of Border Dispute Arbitration with Slovenia" (2015).
[46] Goncalves et al. (2014).

Table 6.15 Slovenia—Nations in Transition Scores (2015)

Nations in Transit Ratings and Averaged Scores										
	2006	2007	2008	2009	2010	2011	2012	2013	2014	2015
Electoral Process	1.50	1.50	1.50	1.50	1.50	1.50	1.50	1.50	1.50	1.50
Civil Society	1.75	2.00	2.00	2.00	2.00	2.00	2.00	2.00	2.00	2.00
Independent Media	1.75	2.00	2.25	2.25	2.25	2.25	2.25	2.25	2.25	2.25
National Democratic Governance	2.00	2.00	2.00	2.00	2.00	2.00	2.00	2.00	2.00	2.00
Local Democratic Governance	1.50	1.50	1.50	1.50	1.50	1.50	1.50	1.50	1.50	1.50
Judicial Framework and Independence	1.50	1.50	1.50	1.75	1.75	1.75	1.75	1.75	1.75	1.75
Corruption	2.25	2.25	2.25	2.50	2.50	2.50	2.25	2.25	2.50	2.50
Democracy Score	1.75	1.82	1.86	1.93	1.93	1.93	1.89	1.89	1.93	1.93

Note: The ratings are based on a scale of 1 to 7, with 1 representing the highest level of democratic progress and 7 the lowest. The democracy score is an average of ratings for the categories tracked in a given year.
Source: The data above are drawn from The World Bank, World Development Indicators 2015.

Further, it is important to recognize that political risk is taking new and different forms in both advanced and emerging economies. This includes dealing with real or perceived income inequality, sovereign debt, state actions to promote state-owned companies, erecting of trade barriers—all of which have the potential pose serious threats to companies.

Businesses increasingly focus their attention on financial, market, and operational forms of risk, particularly in the wake of the 2008 economic crisis. According to a recent Global Risk Management study, most companies neither measure nor manage political risk. Instead, they tend to accept (or ignore) them, or avoid entering situations that post significant risk, even when they might lead to a significant opportunity for growth.[47]

Conclusion

The level of political risk in CEE states reflects the mixture of economic, political, and social progress in reform across the region. On the one hand, political analysts express concern about the growing authoritarian tendencies of regimes in Central Europe and Central Asia. Since 2000, Freedom House reports that the number of "consolidated authoritarian regimes" across both regions has more than doubled. While opponents of democracy are far less powerful in Central and Southeastern Europe, there are notable cases where parties and personalities have emerged with strong antidemocratic rhetoric. This is most evident in Hungary, where media freedom, national democratic governance, and the openness of the electoral process have declined dramatically in the years since Viktor Orbán's and the Fidesz party came to power more than in any country in the same period.

On the other hand, nearly all EU member states in CEE have reformed their governing institutions and created significant protection for civil society organizations and media outlets. Analysts rank Slovenia, Estonia, Latvia, Poland, Czech Republic, Lithuania, and Slovakia as "consolidated democracies," with Hungary, Bulgaria, Romania, Serbia, and

---

[47] Deloitte (2012).

Croatia, and Bosnia and Herzegovina making strides toward consolidation. Despite concerns about partisan friction and influence over media, the Czech Republic continued to see stability and improvement in its new government. Romania escalated a high number of corruption cases, while Slovakia took steps to improve transparency in its judiciary.

References

Alam, A., P.A. Casero, F. Khan, and C. Udomsaph. 2008. *Unleashing Prosperity: Productivity Growth in Eastern Europe and the Former Soviet Union.* Washington: World Bank.

Amadeo, K. November 7, 2013. "What Is a Currency War?" Retrieved from http://useconomy.about.com/od/tradepolicy/g/Currency-Wars.htm

Andrej Kiska. 2015. "NATO2020: We Need Trust, Solidarity, and Resolve." *News Release*, November 11, www.prezident.sk/en/article/prezident-na-nato2020-potrebujeme-doveru-solidaritu-a-rozhodnost/

Aprinķis.lv. March 18, 2014. "Puse Latvijas iedzīvotāju atbalsta NATO militārās klātbūtnes pastiprināšanu [Half of Latvian Citizens Support the NATO Military Presence in the Reinforcement]" Retrieved from www.aprinkis.lv/babites-novads-zinas/latvija/item/16700-puse-latvijas-iedzivotaju-atbalsta-nato-militaras-klatbutnes-pastiprinasanu#

"Apstiprināta jaunā valdība Laimdotas Straujumas vadībā" January 22, 2014 [Approved the new government under management of Laimdota Laimdota], LV portals. http://m.lvportals.lv/visi/galerijas/955-apstiprinata-jauna-valdiba-laimdotas-straujumas-vadiba/

Aristovnik, A. 2006. *The Determinants & Excessiveness of Current Account Deficits in Eastern Europe and the Former Soviet Union.* Retrieved from http://papers.ssrn.com/sol3/papers.cfm?abstract_id=920507 (accessed August 12, 2015).

Arkalgud, A.P. 2011. "Filling 'Institutional Voids' in Emerging Markets." *Forbes Magazine*, September 9. www.forbes.com/sites/infosys/2011/09/20/filling-institutional-voids-in-emerging-markets/ (accessed December 15, 2015).

Bandelji, N. 2007. "Supraterritoriality, Embeddedness, or Both? Foreign Direct Investment in Central and Eastern Europe." In *Globalization: Perspectives from Central and Eastern Europe,* ed. K. Fábián, 25–63. Amsterdam: Jai Press.

Bandelj, N. 2008. *From Communists to Foreign Capitalists: The Social Foundations of Foreign Direct Investment in Postsocialist Europe.* Princeton, NJ: Princeton University Press.

Bartlett, W. 2007. "Economic Restructuring, Job Creation and the Changing Demand for Skills in the Western Balkans." In *Labour Markets in the Western Balkans: Challenges for the Future,* ed. A. Fetsi, 19–50. Turin: European Training Foundation.

Beachain, D., V. Sheridan, and S. Stan. 2012. *Life in Post-Communist Eastern Europe After EU Membership: Happy Ever After?* New York: Routledge.

Bevin, A., and S. Estrin. 2004. "The Determinants of Foreign Direct Investment: An Empirical Analysis." *Journal of Comparative Economics* 32, pp. 775–87.

Bideleux, R., and I. Jeffries. 2007. *A History of Eastern Europe: Crisis and Change.* 2nd ed. London: Routledge.

BIS: Department of Business, Innovation, and Skills. 2010. "The Benefits and Achievements of EU Single Market." UK Government National Archives. Retrieved from http://webarchive.nationalarchives.gov.uk/+/bis.gov.uk/policies/europe/benefits-of-eu-embership (accessed December 28, 2015).

Bornhorst, F., and S. Commander. 2006. "Regional Unemployment and Its Persistence in Transition Countries." *Economics of Transition* 14, no. 2, pp. 269–88.

Brahmbhatt, M., O. Canuto, and S. Ghosh. December 2010. "Currency Wars Yesterday and Today." Economic Premise, The World Bank, Number 43.

Brunwasser, M. 2013. "After Political Appoint in Bulgaria, Rage Boils Over." *The New York Times*, June 28. Retrieved from www.nytimes.com/2013/06/29/world/europe/after-political-appointment-in-bulgaria-rage-boils-over.html?_r=0

"Bulgaria's 2014 Parliamentary Election: CEC Announces Final Results." October 9, 2014. The Sofia Globe, http://sofiaglobe.com/2014/10/09/bulgarias-2014-parliamentary-election-cec-announces-final-results/.

Bukovskis, K., and A. Sprūds. 2015. "Latvia: Nations in Transit 2015." Freedom House. Retrieved from https://freedomhouse.org/report/nations-transit/2015/latvia

Busky, D.F. July 20, 2000. *Democratic Socialism: A Global Survey.* Santa Barbara, CA: Praeger.

Canuto, O. 2010. "Toward a Switchover of Locomotives in the Global Economy." *Economic Premise*, no. 33. Retrieved from www-wds.worldbank.org/external/default/WDSContentServer/WDSP/IB/2010/09/30/000334955_2010093 0035932/Rendered/PDF/568290BRI0EP330Box353739B01PUBLIC1.pdf

Canuto, O., and M. Giugale, eds. 2010. *The Day After Tomorrow—A Handbook on the Future of Economic Policy in the Developing World.* Washington, DC: World Bank.

Case, K.E., and C. Fair. 2004. *Principles of Economics.* Prentice Hall: Pearson.

Crampton, R.J. 1994. *Eastern Europe in the Twentieth Century.* London: Routledge.

"Croatia to Pull Out of Border Dispute Arbitration with Slovenia." 2015. *DW*, July 27. Retrieved from www.dw.com/en/croatia-to-pull-out-of-border-dispute-arbitration-with-slovenia/a-18610325

Cunningham, B. 2015. "Slovakia: Nations in Transit 2015." Freedom House. Retrieved from https://freedomhouse.org/report/nations-transit/2015/slovakia

Cuprik, R. 2014. "Pavol Paška of Smer Resigns." *Slovak Spectator*, November 17. Retrieved from http://spectator.sme.sk/c/20052671/pavol-paska-of-smer-resigns.html

Czech Republic Profile—Leaders. 2015. *BBC News*, December 25. Retrieved from www.bbc.com/news/world-europe-17220320 (accessed December 29, 2015).

Dabrowski, M. December 10, 2014. "Central and eastern Europe: uncertain prospects of economic convergence." Brugel. Retrieved from http://bruegel.org/2014/12/central-and-eastern-europe-uncertain-prospects-of-economic-convergence/

Dabrowski, M. February 2015. "It Is Not Just Russia: Current Crisis in the CIS." Bruegel Policy Contribution, no. 1. Retrieved from http://bruegel.org/wp-content/uploads/imported/publications/pc_2015_01_CIS_.pdf (accessed January 10, 2016).

Dale, G. 2004. *Between State Capitalism and Globalization: The Collapse of the East German Economy*. Oxford: Lang.

Dale, G, ed. 2011. *First the Transition, Then the Crash: Eastern Europe in the 2000s*. London: Pluto Press.

Day, M., and B. Waterfeld. 2014. "Donald Tusk, the New Head of Europe." *The Telegraph*, August 31. Retrieved from www.telegraph.co.uk/news/worldnews/europe/eu/11066174/Donald-Tusk-the-new-head-of-Europe.html

de Crombruggle, A., Z. Minton-Beddoes, and J. Sachs. 1996. *EU Membership for Central Europe: Commitments, Speed, and Conditionality*. Cambridge, MA: Harvard Institute for International Development.

de la Dehesa, G. 2006. *Winners and Losers in Globalization*. Oxford: Blackwell Publishing.

Deloitte. 2012. "Aftershock: Adjusting to the New World of Risk Management." *Forbes: Management and Business Operations*. Retrieved from www.forbes.com/forbesinsights/risk_management_2012/

Derluguian, G. 2005. *Bourdieu's Secret Admirer in the Caucasus: A World System Biography*. Chicago: University of Chicago Press.

Dolan, E. 2012. "What Happened When Poland's Fixed Exchange Rate Experiment Failed: Lessons for a Euro Divorce." *EconoMonitor*. Retrieved from www.economonitor.com/dolanecon/2012/04/13/what-happened-when-polands-fixed-exchange-rate-experiment-failed-lessons-for-a-euro-divorce/#sthash.BGjvEvtE.dpuf

Drahokoupil, J. 2009. *Globalization and the State in Central and Eastern Europe: The Politics of Foreign Direct Investment*. London: Routledge.

Drolc, T. 2015. "Out State Must Become a Promotor of Sustainable Economic Growth and Development." *The Slovenia Times*, December 16. Retrieved from www.sloveniatimes.com/our-state-must-become-a-promotor-of-sustainable-economic-growth-and-development

Du Bois, G., and M. Davidova. 2015. "China and the Czech Republic, a Recent Political Shift." *Nouvelle Europe*, June 29. Retrieved from www.nouvelle-europe.eu/en/china-and-czech-republic-recent-political-shift

Dumbrovsky, T. March 18, 2014. "Constitutional Change through Euro Crisis Law: A Multi-Level Legal Analysis." European University Institute. Retrieved from http://eurocrisislaw.eui.eu/slovakia/

Dzidic, D. 2014. "Bosnia-Herzegovina Hit by Wave of Violent Protests." *The Guardian*, February 7. Retrieved from www.theguardian.com/world/2014/feb/07/bosnia-herzegovina-wave-

The Economist's Writers. 2013. "Taking Europe's Pulse." *The Economist*, November 05. www.economist.com/blogs/graphicdetail/2013/11/european-economy-guide (accessed December 13, 2013).

ETF. 2011. *Labour Markets and Employability: Trends and Challenges in Armenia, Azerbaijan, Belarus, Georgia, Moldova and Ukraine.* Turin: European Training Foundation.

The European Union Explained: Economic and Monetary Union and the Euro. 2014. Luxembourg: European Commission Publication.

European Commission. 1993. "Copenhagen Criteria." Retrieved from http://europa.eu/rapid/press-release_DOC-93-3_en.htm?locale=en

European Commission. January 21, 2014. "President Barroso Meets Serbian Prime Minister Dačić." Retrieved from http://europa.eu/rapid/press-release_IP-14-52_en.htm

Faber, A. 2009. "The effects of Enlargement on the European Polity: State of the Art and Theoretical and Methodological Challenges." In *Enlarging the European Union: Effects on the New Member States and the EU*, eds, G. Avery, A. Faber, and A. Schmidt, 20–28. Brussels: Trans European Policy Studies Association. Retrieved from www.um.edu.mt/__data/assets/pdf_file/0017/71054/Enlarging_the_European_Union.

Feige, E. 1991. "Perestroika and Ruble Convertibility." *Cato Journal* 10, no. 3, pp. 631–53. Retrieved from http://object.cato.org/sites/cato.org/files/serials/files/cato-journal/1991/1/cj10n3-2.pdf (accessed September 12, 2015).

Feige, E. 1994. "The Transition to a Market Economy in Russia: Property Rights, Mass Privatization and Stabilization." In *A Fourth Way?: Privatization, Property, and the Emergence of New Market Economics*, eds. G. Alexander and G. Skąpska, 57–78. London: Routledge.

G.K. 2014. "Romania and Bulgaria: Depressing Reading." *The Economist: Eastern Approaches,* January 22. Retrieved from www.economist.com/blogs/easternapproaches/2014/01/romania-and-bulgaria

Global Edge. n.d. "Serbia: Introduction." Michigan State University. Retrieved from http://globaledge.msu.edu/countries/serbia (accessed November 24, 2015).

Goclowski, M., and P. Florkiewicz. 2015. "Polish President Suffers Shock Reverse in First Round Vote: Exit Poll." *Reuters*, May 10. Retrieved from www.reuters.com/article/2015/05/11/us-poland-vote-president-idUSKBN0NU0RX20150511

Goncalves, M., Jose Alves, Carlos Frota, Harry Xia, and Rajabahadur V. Arcot. 2014. "Coping with Political and Economic Risks." *Advanced Economies and Emerging Markets: Prospects for Globalization*, 298–99. New York: Business Expert Press.

Green, F., D. Ashton, D. James, and J. Sung. 1999a. "The Role of the State in Skill Formation: Evidence from the Republic of Korea, Singapore, and Taiwan." *Oxford Review of Economic Policy* 15, no. 1, pp. 82–96.

Green, F., D. James, D. Ashton, and J. Sung. 1999b. "Post-School Education and Training Policy in Development States: The Cases of Taiwan and South Korea." *Journal of Education Policy* 14, no. 3, pp. 301–15.

Gros, D., and A. Steinherr. 1995. *Winds of Change: Economic Transition in Central and Eastern Europe*. London: Longman.

Guerrera, F. 2013. "Currency War Has Started." *The Wall Street Journal*, February 04. http://online.wsj.com/news/articles/SB10001424127887324761004578283684195892250 (accessed December 13, 2013).

Guyader, M. 2009. "Accession Effects on Cohesion in the New Member States." In *Enlarging the European Union: Effects on the New Member States and the EU*, eds. G. Avery, A. Faber, and A. Schmidt, 101–3. Brussels: Trans European Policy Studies Association. Retrieved from www.um.edu.mt/__data/assets/pdf_file/0017/71054/Enlarging_the_European_Union.pdf

Haynes, M., and R. Hasan. 1998. "The State and Market in the Transition Economies: Critical Remarks in the Light of Past History and the Current Experience." *The Journal of European Economic History* 27, no. 3, pp. 609–46.

Heinisch, R., and C. Landsberger. 2012. "Returning to Europe: East Central Europe's Complex Relationship with European Integration and its Repercussions." In *The Routledge History of East Central Europe Since 1700*, eds. A.S. Klimo and I. Livezeanu. Retrieved from www.uni-salzburg.at/fileadmin/multimedia/Politikwissenschaft%20und%20Soziologie/documents/Heinisch-Landsberger_East_Central_Europe%E2%80%99s_Complex_Relationship_with_European_Integration.pdf

Hinsburg, H., J. Matt, and R. Vinni. 2015. "Estonia: Nations in Transit." Freedom House. Retrieved from https://freedomhouse.org/report/nations-transit/2015/estonia

Hirsch, D., J. Kett, and J. Trefil. 2002. *The New Dictionary of Cultural Literacy.* Boston: Houghton Mifflin Harcourt.

Hoogvelt, A. 1997. *Globalization and the Postcolonial World.* Basingstoke: Macmillan.

HRW. 2014. "World Report 2014: Turkmenistan." Retrieved from www.hrw. org/world-report/2014/country-chapters/turkmenistan (accessed January 28, 2016).

Human Rights First. October 17, 2014. "U.S. Sanctions Target Corrupt Hungarian Officials."

Human Rights Watch, World Report. 2015. "Kazakhstan." Retrieved from www. humanrightsfirst.org/press-release/us-sanctions-target-corrupt-hungarian-officials (accessed January 28, 2016).

Humer, Ž. 2007. "Europeanization and the Equal Opportunities Policy in Slovenia" In *Globalization: Perspectives from Central and Eastern Europe,* ed. K. Fábián, 305–26. Oxford: JAI Press.

IMF. 1997. *World Economic Outlook.* Washington, DC: International Monetary Fund. Retrieved from www.imf.org/external/pubs/ft/weo/weo1097/weocon97.htm

IMF. 2010a. *World Economic Outlook.* Washington, DC: International Monetary Fund. Retrieved from www.imf.org/external/pubs/ft/weo/2010/01/index.htm

IMF. 2014. *Central, Eastern, and Southeastern Europe: Regional Economic Issues Update.* Washington, DC: International Monetary Fund. Retrieved from www.imf.org/external/pubs/ft/reo/2014/eur/eng/pdf/erei1014.pdf

Index of Economic Freedom: Estonia. 2015. "The Heritage Foundation." Retrieved from www.heritage.org/index/country/estonia

The Independent. January 28, 1994. "The UNICEF Annual Report." Retrieved from www.unicef.org/about/history/files/unicef_annual_report_1994.pdf

IndustryWeek. April 9, 2008. "Slovak Car Industry Production Almost Doubled in 2007." Industryweek.com. Retrieved from www.industryweek.com/global-economy/slovak-car-industry-production-almost-doubled-2007 (accessed October 10, 2015).

Iossifov, P. 2015. "Disinflation in Non-Eurozone EU Nations." VOX CEPR Policy Portal. Retrieved from www.voxeu.org/article/disinflation-non-eurozone-eu-nations (accessed January 10, 2016).

Jacoby, W. 2004. *The Enlargement of the European Union and NATO: Ordering from the Menu in Central Europe.* Cambridge, UK: Cambridge University Press.

Jahan, S. March 28, 2012. "Inflation Targeting: Holding the Line." *Finance & Development.*

Jensen, N. October 2008. "Political Risk, Democratic Institutions, and Foreign Direct Investment." *The Journal of Politics* 70, no. 4, pp. 1040–52.

Jones, M. 2015. "Central Europe Looking Tranquil Port in Emerging Markets Storm." *Reuters,* August 10. Retrieved from http://finance.yahoo. com/news/central-europe-looking-tranquil-port-124848904.html;_ ylt=A0LEVrciwMhV52gAqLMnnIlQ;_ylu=X3oDMTByMjB0aG5zB GNvbG8DYmYxBHBvcwMxBHZ0aWQDBHNlYwNzYw

K.S. 2013. "Resignation Amid Scandal." *The Economist: Eastern Approaches,* June 18.

Kajne, S. 2009. "The Effects of EU Enlargement: Slovenia." In *Enlarging the European Union: Effects on the New Member States and the EU,* eds. G. Avery, A. Faber, and A. Schmidt. Brussels, Belgium: Trans European Policy Studies Association.

Khanna, T., and K.G. Palepu. 2010. *Winning in Emerging Markets: A Roadmap for Strategy and Execution.* Boston: Harvard Business School Publishing.

Kapacki, R., and M. Prochiniak. 2009. "The EU Enlargement and the Economic Growth in the CEE New Member Countries." European Commission, Brussels. Retrieved from http://ec.europa.eu/economy_finance/publications/ publication14295_en.pdf (accessed January 10, 2016).

Karasinka-Fendler, M. 2009. "The Effects of Accession on Poland." In *Enlarging the European Union: Effects on the New Member States and the EU,* eds. G. Avery, A. Faber, and A. Schmidt. Trans European Policy Studies Association.

Kaza, J. 2015. "Latvia's Prime Minister Laimdota Straujuma Steps Down." *Wall Street Journal,* December 5. Retrieved from www.wsj.com/articles/latvias-premier-laimdota-straujuma-steps-down-1449480185

Kolev, A., and C. Saget. 2005. "Understanding Youth Labour Market Disadvantage: Evidence from South-East Europe." *International Labour Review* 144, no. 2, p. 161.

Kornecki, L. 2010. "Foreign Direct Investment and Macroeconomic Changes in CEE Integrating in to the Global Market." *Journal of International Business and Cultural Studies.* Embry-Riddle Aeronautical University. Retrieved from www.aabri.com/manuscripts/09222.pdf (accessed January 08, 2016).

Krassimir, N.Y., and S.D. Kaloyan. 2009. "The Effects of EU Accession on Bulgaria." In *Enlarging the European Union: Effects on the New Member States and the EU,* eds. G. Avery, A. Faber, and A. Schmidt. Trans European Policy Studies Association.

Kunštát, D. November 2015. Důvěra stranickým představitelům [Confidence in Party Representatives], Centrum pro výzkum veřejného mínění [Public Opinion Research Center] (Prague: CVVM). http://cvvm.soc.cas.cz/en/ politicians-political-institutions/confidence-in-constitutional-institutions-and-satisfaction-with-political-situation-in-november-2015

Kuruvilla, S., C.L. Erickson, and A. Hwang. 2002. "An Assessment of the Singapore Skills Development System: Does It Constitute a Viable Model for Other Developing Countries?" *World Development* 30, no. 8, pp. 1461–76.

Leconte, C. 2010. *Understanding Euroscepticism*. Basingstoke, MD: Palgrave MacMillan.

Lejour A.M., and R. Nahuis. 2004. "EU Accession and the Catching Up of the Central and East European Countries." In *The Past, Present and Future of the European Union*, ed. A. Deardorff, IEA Conference Volume, no. 138. New York: Palgrave Macmillan.

Lonely Planet. n.d. "Lonely Planet's Bosnia and Herzegovina Tourism Profile." www.lonelyplanet.com/bosnia-and-hercegovina (accessed January 02, 2016).

Lsm.lv. July 2014. "Budžeta komisija apstiprina aizsardzības finansējuma pieauguma grafiku" [Budgetary Commission approves defense funding growth schedule]. www.lsm.lv/lv/raksts/latvija/zinas/budzheta-komisija-apstiprina-aizsardziibas-finansejuma-pieauguma.a90189/

Mardiste, D. 2015. "Pro-Russian Estonia Mayor Arrested for Bribery." *Reuters*, September 22. Retrieved from www.reuters.com/article/us-estonia-arrest-idUSKCN0RM1R820150922

McKinnon, R.I. 1973. *Money and Capital in Economic Development*. Washington, DC: Brookings Institution.

Medrano, J.D. 2003. *Framing Europe: Attitudes toward European Integration in Germany, Spain, and the United Kingdom*. Princeton, NJ: Princeton University Press.

Meyer, K. 1995. "Foreign Direct Investment in the Early Years of Economic Transition: A Survey." *Economics of Transition* 2, pp. 301–20.

Meyer, K. 1998. *Direct Investment in Economies in Transition*. Massachusetts: Edward Elgar.

Moghadam, R., R. Teja, and P. Berkmen. 2014. "Euro Area Deflation Versus Lowflation." iMFdirect blog. Retrieved from http://blog-imfdirect.imf.org/2014/03/04/euro-area-deflation-versus-lowflation/ (accessed January 10, 2016).

Moore, J.B. 1969. *Social Origins of Dictatorship in Democracy*. Harmondsworth: Penguin.

Mráz, P. 2015. "Reforming the Czech Civil Service: An Unfinished Journey." *Post*. Retrieved from http://postnito.cz/reforming-the-czech-civil-service-an-unfinished-journey/ (accessed December 29, 2015).

Mühlberger, M., and K. Körner. 2014. "CEE: Fit for the Next Decade in the EU." EU Monitor, Deutsche Bank. Retrieved from www.dbresearch.com/PROD/DBR_INTERNET_EN-PROD/PROD0000000000333559/CEE%3A+Fit+for+the+next++decade+in+the+EU.pdf (accessed January 03, 2016).

Nardelli, A, D. Dzidic, and E. Jukic. 2014. "Bosnia and Herzegovnia: The World's Most Complicated System of Government?" *The Guardian*, October 8. Retrieved from www.theguardian.com/news/datablog/2014/oct/08/bosnia-herzegovina-elections-the-worlds-most-complicated-system-of-government

Newell, A., and F. Pastore. 2006. "Regional Unemployment and Its Persistence in Transition Countries." *Economics of Transition* 14, no. 2, pp. 269–88.

Novinite.com. January 16, 2015. "Bulgaria to Follow Romanian Example in Fighting Corruption – Deputy PM." Retrieved from www.novinite.com/articles/166000/Bulgaria+to+Follow+Romanian+Example+in+Fighting+Corruption+%E2%80%93+Deputy+PM

OECD. 1998. "Survey of OECD Work on International Investment." Organization for Economic Co-Operation and Development. Working Paper. https://www.oecd.org/investment/investment-policy/WP-1998_1.pdf

OECD. 2015. "Central and Eastern Europe, the Caucasus and Central Asia." Retrieved from www.iea.org/newsroomandevents/pressreleases/2015/april/iea-reviews-energy-policies-countries-in-eastern-europe-caucasus-central-asia.html (accessed September 12, 2015).

Özsagir, A., and Y. Bayraktutan. 2010. "The Relationship Between Vocational Education and Industrial Production in Turkey." *International Journal of Economic Perspectives* 4, no. 2, pp. 439–48.

Outhwaite, W. 2010. "What Is Left After 1989?" In *The Global 1989: Continuity and Change in World Politics,* eds. G. Lawson, C. Armbruster and M. Cox. Cambridge: Cambridge University Press.

Pacek, N., and D. Thorniley. 2007. *Eastern Europe Markets: Lessons for Business and the Outlook for Different Markets.* 2nd ed. London: The Economist and Profile Books.

Petrolongo, B., and C. Pissarides. 2001. "Looking Into the Black Box: A Survey of the Matching Function." *Journal of Economic Literature* 39, pp. 390–431.

Pitas, C. 2015. "Jaguar Land Rover Plans New Plant in Slovakia." *Reuters,* August 11. ed. J. Merriman. Retrieved from www.reuters.com/article/jaguar-lndrover-slovakia-idUSL5N1033QE20150811#bW9TkFRo3BsYJTmT.97 (accessed September 20, 2014).

Pleso, S. 2014. "Fico's Suprising Defeat." *The Economist* March 31. Retrieved from www.economist.com/blogs/easternapproaches/2014/03/slovakias-election-0

"Police Search Home of Former Slovenian Premier." 2015. *Daily Mail,* March 11. Retrieved from www.dailymail.co.uk/wires/ap/article-2989681/Police-search-home-former-Slovenian-premier.html

R.P. April 3, 2015. "A New State Body to Fight Corruption in Bulgaria." CEE Insight. Retrieved from www.ceeinsight.net/2015/04/03/new-state-body-fight-corruption-bulgaria/

Radka Minecherová. 2014. "Slovakia Improves on the Corruption Index." *Slovak Spectator,* December 3. Retrieved from http://spectator.sme.sk/articles/view/56140/10/slovakia_improves_in_the_corruption_index.html

Reinhart, C.M., and J.F. Kirkegaard. 2012. "Financial Repression: Then and Now." Voxeu. Retrieved from www.voxeu.org/article/financial-repression-then-and-now (accessed April 23, 2012).

Resolution of the European Council on the Stability and Growth Pact Amsterdam. June 17, 1997. Retrieved from http://eur-lex.europa.eu/legal-content/EN/ALL/?uri=CELEX:31997Y0802%2801%29

Reuters. 2013. "OECD Sees Economic Rebound in CEE, Russia in 2015." Retrieved from www.reuters.com/article/oecd-economy-east-idUSL5N0J33P820131119 (accessed January 02, 2016).

Roaf, J., R. Atoyan, B. Joshi, and K. Krogulski. October 2014. "25 Years of Transition: Post-Communist Europe and the IMF." *International Monetary Fund,* p. 15.

"Romania Supports Sanctions Against Russia Until Full Implementation of Minsk Agreements." 2015. *Unian,* March 17. Retrieved from www.unian.info/politics/1056476-romania-supports-sanctions-against-russia-until-full-implementation-of-minsk-agreements.html

Rozmahel, P., L. Kouba, L. Grochová, and N. Najman. 2013. "Integration of Central and Eastern European Countries: Increasing EU Heterogeneity?" European Commission, WWWforEurope, Working Paper no. 9, Retrieved from www.foreurope.eu/fileadmin/documents/pdf/Workingpapers/WWWfor Europe_WPS_no009_MS77.pdf (accessed January 10, 2016).

Sachs, J. 1994. *Poland's Jump to the Market Economy.* Cambridge, MA: M.I.T. Press.

Schadler, S., P. Drummond, L. Kuijs, Z. Murgasova, and R. Van Elkan. 2005. *Adopting the Euro in Central Europe: Challenges of the Next Step in European Integration.* Washington, DC: International Monetary Fund.

Schmidt, K.D. 1995. "Foreign Direct Investment in Eastern Europe: State-of-the-Art and Prospects." In *Transforming economies and European Integration,* eds. R. Dobrinsky and M. Lndesmann, 268–89. Aldershot, UK: Edward Elgar.

"Serbian Prime Minister Vucic Pledges Millions to Srebrenica." 2015. *DW,* November 11. Retrieved from www.dw.com/en/serbian-prime-minister-vucic-pledges-millions-to-srebrenica/a-18843982

Serbos, S. 2008. "European Integration and South Eastern Europe: Prospects and Challenges for the Western Balkans." *UNISCI Discussion Papers* 18, p. 97.

Shields, S. 2011. "Poland the Global Political Economy: From Neoliberalism to Populism (And Back Again)." In *First the Transition, Then the Crash: Eastern Europe in the 2000s,* ed. G. Dale, 169–86. London: Pluto Press.

Sjöberg, Ö., and M. Wyzan, eds. 1991. *Economic Change in the Balkan States.* London: Pinter.

Skrpec, D. September 11, 2015. "Playing the Field in Serbia." Foreign Affairs. Retrieved from www.foreignaffairs.com/articles/serbia/2015-09-11/playing-field-serbia

"Slovenia Prime Minister Alenka Bratusek Resigns." 2014. *DW,* May 5. Retrieved from www.dw.com/en/slovenia-prime-minister-alenka-bratusek-resigns/a-17612637

Smith, A. 2000. *The Return to Europe: The Reintegration of Eastern Europe into the European Economy.* London, UK: Palgrave MacMillan.

Smith-Doerr, L., and W. Powell. 2005. "Networks and Economic Life." In *The Handbook of Economic Sociology,* eds. N. Smelser and R. Swedberg, 379–402. 2nd ed. Princeton, NJ: Princeton University Press.

"Šogad Krievijas bruņoto spēku lidmašīnas un kuģi Latvijai pietuvojušies vairāk nekā 250 reizes." December 1, 2014. [This Year, the Russian Military Planes and Ships Have Approached Latvia More Than 250 Times], LETA/Tvnet. lv. Retrieved from www.tvnet.lv/zinas/latvija/537513-sogad_krievijas_ brunoto_speku_lidmasinas_un_kugi_latvijai_pietuvojusies_vairak_ neka_250_reizes

Sommers, J., and J. Bērziņš. 2011. "Twenty Years Lost: Latvia's Failed Development in the Post-Soviet World." In *First the Transition, Then the Crash: Eastern Europe in the 2000s,* ed. G. Dale, 119–42. London: Pluto Press.

Sondergaard, L., and M. Murthi. 2012. *Skills, Not Just Diplomas: Managing Education for Results in Eastern Europe and Central Asia.* Washington: The World Bank.

Stoian, C. April 8–9, 2005. "Multinationals in Emerging Markets: Making the Best of the Good Side: Comparative Evidence from Poland and Romania." Paper at the Academy of International Business Conference. UK Chapter, Bath.

Stokes, G., ed. 1991. *From Stalinism to Pluralism.* Oxford: Oxford University Press.

Svensson, L.E.O. 2008. "Inflation Targeting." In *The New Palgrave Dictionary of Economics,* eds. S.N. Durlauf, and L.E. Blume. 2nd ed. New York: Palgrave Macmillan.

Szemler, T. 2009. "The Effects of Accession in Hungary." In *Enlarging the European Union: Effects on the New Member States and the EU,* eds. G. Avery, A. Faber, and A. Schmidt. Brussels, Belgium: Trans European Policy Studies Association.

Taggart, P. 1998. "A. Touchstone of Dissent: Euroscepticism in Contemporary Western European Party Systems." *European Journal of Political Research* 33, no. 3, pp. 363–88.

Tamás, G.M. 2011. "Marx on 1989." In *First the Transition, Then the Crash: Eastern Europe in the 2000s,* ed. G. Dale, 21–48. London: Pluto Press.

Taras, R., ed. 1992. *The Road to Disillusion: From Critical Marxism to Postcommunism in Eastern Europe.* Armonk, NY: M.E. Sharpe.

Terenzani-Stankova, M. 2014. "Still No Deal on Reporting Property." *Slovak Spectator*, October 6. Retrieved from http://spectator.sme.sk/articles/view/55446/2/still_no_deal_on_reporting_property.html

Thomann, A. 2006. "Skype, a Baltic Success Story." Retrieved from www.credit-suisse.com/us/en/news-and-expertise/economy/articles/news-and-expertise/2006/09/en/skype-a-baltic-success-story.html, 02/24/2008 (accessed December 12, 2015).

Transparency International. 2014. "Corruption Perceptions Index 2014." Berlin. Retrieved from www.transparency.org/country#SVK_DataResearch_SurveysIndices

"Treaty of Maastricht on European Union." n.d. *European Union Law*. Retrieved from http://eur-lex.europa.eu/legal-content/EN/TXT/?uri =URISERV:xy0026 (accessed July 7, 2015).

Tupy, M.L. September 2003. "EU Enlargement: Costs, Benefits, and Strategies for Central and Eastern European Countries." *Policy Analysis Review* 489. p. 4.

Ummelas, O. 2011. "In Eastern Europe, Cold Feet About Joining the Euro." *Bloomberg Business*, June 23. Retrieved from www.bloomberg.com/bw/magazine/content/11_27/b4235017725502.htm

UNCTAD (United Nations Conference on Trade and Development). 1998. *World Investment Report*. Washington, DC: United Nations Conference on Trade and Development.

UNCTAD. 2006. http://unctadstat.unctad.org/wds/TableViewer/tableView.aspx

van Brabant, J.M. 1989. *Economic Integration in Eastern Europe*. London: Harvester Wheatsheaf.

V.V.B. 2013. "Breaking up With Peevski." *The Economist: Eastern Approaches*, September 20.

"Vyriausybės Naujienlaiškis." June 2, 2014. [Government Newsletter Nr. 125 (22)]. Retrieved from http://lrv.lt/naujienos/savaites-naujienos/?nid=14508

Walton, J., and D. Seddon. 1994. *Free Markets and Food Riots: The Politics of Global Adjustment*. Oxford: Blackwell.

Whitefield, S., and R. Rohrschneider. 2006. "Forum Section. Political parties, Public Opinion and European Integration in Post-Communist Countries. The State of the Art." *European Union Politics* 7, no. 1, pp. 141–60.

Wolchik, S.L., and J.L. Curry. 2011. *Central and East European Politics: From Communism to Democracy*. Lanham, MD: Rowman & Littlefield Publishers.

Zaman, G. 2008. "Economic Effects of CEE Countries Integration into the European Union." *Journal Annales Universitatis Apulensis Series Oeconomica* 2, no. 10, p. 2.

Index

OTHER TITLES FROM THE ECONOMICS COLLECTION
Philip Romero, The University of Oregon and
Jeffrey Edwards, North Carolina A&T State University, Editors

- *Macroeconomics: Integrating Theory, Policy and Practice for a New Era* by David G. Tuerck
- *Emerging and Frontier Markets: The New Frontline for Global Trade* by Marcus Goncalves and Jose Alves
- *Doing Business in Emerging Markets: Roadmap for Success* by Marcus Goncalves, Jose Alves, and Rajabahadur V. Arcot
- *Seeing the Future: How to Build Basic Forecasting Models* by Tam Bang Vu
- *U.S. Politics and the American Macroeconomy* by Gerald T. Fox
- *Global Public Health Policies: Case Studies from India on Planning and Implementation* by KV Ramani
- *How Strong is Your Firm's Competitive Advantage, Second Edition* by Daniel Marburger
- *Statistics for Economics, Second Edition* by Shahdad Naghshpour
- *Regression for Economics, Second Edition* by Shahdad Naghshpour

Announcing the Business Expert Press Digital Library
Concise e-books business students need for classroom and research

This book can also be purchased in an e-book collection by your library as

- a one-time purchase,
- that is owned forever,
- allows for simultaneous readers,
- has no restrictions on printing, and
- can be downloaded as PDFs from within the library community.

Our digital library collections are a great solution to beat the rising cost of textbooks. E-books can be loaded into their course management systems or onto students' e-book readers. The **Business Expert Press** digital libraries are very affordable, with no obligation to buy in future years. For more information, please visit **www.businessexpertpress.com/librarians**. To set up a trial in the United States, please email **sales@businessexpertpress.com**.

CPSIA information can be obtained
at www.ICGtesting.com
Printed in the USA
FFOW03n1314240217
32840FF